VACANT THRONES

The Author

VACANT THRONES

A VOLUME OF POLITICAL PORTRAITS

BY

SIR IAN MALCOLM

Essay Index Reprint Series

BOOKS FOR LIBRARIES PRESS, INC.

FREEPORT, NEW YORK

First published 1931
Reprinted 1967

LIBRARY OF CONGRESS CATALOG CARD NUMBER:

67-28760

PRINTED IN THE UNITED STATES OF AMERICA

THIS VOLUME IS DEDICATED
WITH
FILIAL VENERATION
TO
THE MOTHER OF PARLIAMENTS

PREFACE

I ADMIT that some reason or excuse is necessary to justify the publication of the following series of personal sketches. Let the one or the other be found in an experience of my own : that in reading history or biography I have often wished that the authors of these important works had been at more pains to give some intimacy as well as publicity to the characters with whom they were dealing, in order that the reader might recon- struct for himself an individual conception of the personages whose lives or policies or achievements were, for the moment, under consideration. Such details are of quite subsidiary importance to the scholar or the student ; but to me, and to other readers in our own libraries, they give light to the eyes, movement to the hands, and direction to the character of the man or woman whose physical and moral outlines we are anxious to recapture.

To our finite minds the invisible is difficult to seize and to retain. Wherefore we need not charge ourselves with lack of faith or with idle curiosity when we confess that we wish it had been possible for us to know something of the physical linea- ments of Our Lord : whether He was tall or

short, clean-shaven or bearded; what His voice
sounded like, what were His amusements and His
tastes. And so, down the centuries, probably every
one of us has felt, with regard to particular characters in history, that our impressions of them
would have been humanised and deepened if we
had been in possession of such details as I have
suggested. For instance, I should like to have in
my mind an accurate idea of Joan of Arc in the
flesh; but, when I go to the museum at Orleans,
I see scores upon scores of so-called portraits of
the Maid, engravings and statuettes and enamels,
no two of which bear the least resemblance to one
another. And of Mary Queen of Scots : but she
is in the same case; for the dozen " likenesses "
that I possess of her vary in every essential trait. Of
Queen Elizabeth's face and figure I thought I had a
final impression, gathered from innumerable portraits attributed to Zucchero; but now that great
authority, the late Sir Lionel Cust, informs us that
a large number of the representations of the Virgin
Queen which we have seen were neither by
Zucchero nor of Her Majesty, but portraits by
other artists of ladies of her Court. All of which
is to be deplored; but it goes to show that if we
cannot trust to brush or pencil for the information
that we crave about many great figures of the past
until about the Eighteenth Century, and that we
are, owing to a lack of family chronicles or gossip

VISCOUNT ESHER

until about the same date, equally short of recorded personal details concerning them, we miss a great deal of agreeable knowledge which it would have been to our advantage to possess.

It is because Boswell and Creevey and Walpole and Greville have done so much to make the society in which they moved live for future generations that we owe them a lasting debt of gratitude; and we could wish that the biographers of to-day would endeavour to take colours from the palettes of Housman and Guedalla, of Lytton Strachey, or of Lord Esher (in " Cloud-capped Towers ") to illustrate the lives which they record.

A very redeeming feature of the journalism of to-day, both in type and in caricature, is that it does seize upon personal idiosyncracies, for whatever their passing worth may be; and writers of biography would be well advised to consult newspaper files as well as State papers when preparing their canvas for a literary portrait. The twirling of Winston Churchill's finger-ring (like the flick of Disraeli's cambric handkerchief) in moments of boredom or excitement must not be left out; nor the yawns (in the grand manner) of Squire Chaplin, nor the snuff-taking of T. P. O'Connor. These are as essential to the true portrait as were Napoleon's forelock, Mr. Gladstone's collars, Lord Randolph Churchill's moustaches, Mr. Joseph Chamberlain's eye-glass and orchid, or Lord Birkenhead's cigar.

For the art of Biography I have the greatest respect; in its perusal I take the greatest pleasure; before its difficulties I have always recoiled. Yet, in the hope that once more the mouse may assist the lion, I have prepared this book of sketches. They are no more than personal memories of vanished friends and acquaintances with whom I have been associated in work or play. If I have at all succeeded in catching a likeness here and there, in discovering a quality that has lain undetected hitherto, and above all in writing so many pages on personal subjects without distorting a character or making an enemy, I shall be well content.

IAN MALCOLM.

CONTENTS

LIST OF ILLUSTRATIONS

NOTE

I am greatly indebted to those who have provided me with the foregoing illustrations, and desire to offer to all of them my warmest thanks.

Lady Salisbury allows me to reproduce the portrait of the late Lord Salisbury; Lady Londonderry that of her father, Lord Chaplin; Lady Harcourt the picture of Lord Harcourt with his daughters; Mrs. Carnegie the snapshot of Mr. Chamberlain; Miss Haldane sends me one of her brother, and Mrs. Alfred Lyttelton the portrait of her late husband. To the Duke of Devonshire I am obliged for the picture of his predecessor; to the Duke of Westminster for the study of Mr. George Wyndham; to Lord Goschen for the sketch of his father, and to Lady Oxford for the likeness of Mr. Asquith.

I feel sure that those who read this little book will share my gratitude to all whom I have mentioned as also to the professional photographers whose work I have been allowed to reproduce in the following pages.

IAN M.

LORD SALISBURY

1830–1903

I WAS brought up, in the best tradition of an old Tory family, to think as badly as possible of Mr. Gladstone, and to believe that nothing but a double dose of Lord Salisbury as Prime Minister and forty years of resolute government would produce tranquillity in Ireland, and restore to Great Britain the prestige which she had lost between 1880 and 1885. It was in July of 1889 that I first saw a Prime Minister of England. I had just come down from Oxford and was walking through St. James's Park when I noticed a tall, heavy, bent and bearded figure standing against the railings and gazing intently across the ornamental water, but apparently gazing at nothing in particular. He was dressed in a roomy black frock-coat and wearing a somewhat rugged tall-hat; he gave me the impression of an Atlas in modern dress, bearing upon his shoulders the weight and the cares of a world-wide Empire. Of course I had realised who he was, for his photographs and caricatures in the newspapers had made Lord Salisbury a familiar figure to the public; and I followed him in distant reverence as far as the park entrance into the

Foreign Office where he slowly disappeared from view.

Within a few years (1895) thanks to a combination of favouring friends and circumstances, I had become his parliamentary private secretary under the careful tuition of Eric Barrington in the Foreign Office and of Schomberg (" Pom ") McDonnell, who were at that time the principal Private Secretaries to the Prime Minister. And so it came about that, during the following five years, I was a constant visitor—either official or unofficial—at Hatfield, and saw something at close quarters of one of the greatest, if not the greatest, public men of my time. As a statesman it was his massiveness and his supremely English qualities which impressed me most as a young man, and which impress me still. He was, in official business, Olympian and aloof ; he was deliberate in reflection and then inspiringly decided ; once determined, he was rapid in action which he could defend in language that was bold, bantering or caustic, as the occasion demanded. His political opponents were fond of charging him from time to time with " blazing indiscretions " of speech ; and even some of the more timid of his supporters professed themselves embarrassed by an occasional phrase of his on the platform or in the House of Lords that laid bare the naked truth of a situation or of a dangerous policy as by a flash of lightning which not infrequently burned as well.

But nobody could lay to Lord Salisbury's charge the objection so often sustained against his great antagonist, Mr. Gladstone—that he used words to dissemble his meaning. For his meaning was as clear as a clarion to all who had ears to hear. " Blazing " it undoubtedly was at times ; but never " indiscreet," in the sense that the speaker had not fully calculated both the necessity for his declaration and the effect that would be produced by the phrase selected to embody it.

The clarity and courage of Lord Salisbury's mind were made manifest very notably in the minutes which he used to append in red ink to despatches for the guidance of his subordinates in the F.O. I hope that some day it may be possible to publish a collection of these to indicate the workings of a great and cautious mind. Many of them I saw during my apprenticeship, and I was deeply impressed by their sagacity ; but, alas, I have only retained the words of one of them. There was question of a Missionary Society sending some of its devoted evangelists into a dangerous and remote part of China to which it was most inexpedient, in the circumstances, that they should proceed. Short of absolutely forbidding them to undertake this perilous journey, everything had been done by the Foreign Office to dissuade them from so doing. Lord Salisbury's intense interest in foreign missions was widely known, but his horror of punitive expeditions, with all that they might entail, remained to be shown. The following minute, written in his own beautiful script, showed it : " It is all very well to have the Gospel of Christ at your head ; but your influence will be greatly diminished if you must be followed by gun-boats at your tail." The calm wisdom of this dictum from a devoted Christian statesman had its immediate effect, and the expedition was deflected elsewhere.

Lord Salisbury's tenure of the Foreign Office will always be regarded, I expect, as one of exceptional brilliancy. And this leads one to wonder whether it is so necessary as is sometimes supposed that a Foreign Minister should be intimately acquainted by personal travel with the countries with which he has to deal. He, of course, had in his youth gone far afield to Australia and New Zealand, but since then his foreign excursions had been mainly confined to France. I remember that Cecil Rhodes told me once at dinner at George Wyndham's, on returning from an interview with Lord Salisbury at the Foreign Office, that he was amazed at the Foreign Minister's knowledge. I can hear him now, saying in his high-pitched voice : " It seemed to me quite extraordinary that such a man, who never travels abroad further than Dieppe or the Riviera, should have found out all the places in South Africa where an Englishman can breed, reserved them for Great Britain, and rejected all the others."

As a leader of the Conservative party he was incomparable, both in Parliament and in the country. It must be remembered that Lord Beaconsfield had accustomed Conservatives to be guided by the inspiration of an inscrutable Sphinx. Lord Salisbury was far less oracular and mysterious than Lord Beaconsfield, but he had that certain aloofness which, in those days, both parties liked in their leaders ; his character and long political career had gained for him a quality of confidence from his Sovereign and from his supporters which nothing could shake. And so it happened that from 1886 to 1902 he was the Chief of an undivided and popular party ; whilst for the whole of that long period (with the exception of the years 1892–1895) he was Prime Minister of England.

And yet I do not suppose that, during the whole of that time, he would have claimed, or that any-one would have claimed for him, the attribute of " popularity " in the sense which we give to that word to-day. He was too reserved to be popular in that sense ; indeed he might have mistrusted himself, as well as those who offered it to him, if he had achieved it. But he was more than popular ; he was an institution in the country ; one whose speeches and despatches were treated with respect by all parties, whether they agreed or disagreed with him, and whose character soared by itself above the rivalries of lesser men. He lived before the days of nicknames, even of initials, and he never was known in public or in private except as Lord Salisbury; it would have seemed almost irreverent to refer to him by any other name, as sacrilegious as to give a soubriquet to St. Paul's Cathedral. I remember once, in connection with this fact, a stinging rebuke being administered by an old member of Parliament to a young one who presumed to say, standing before the fireplace in the *No* lobby of the House of Commons, that "Arthur" (meaning Mr. Balfour, with whom he was but slightly acquainted) had expressed a certain opinion.

"Did he?" said the hot-tempered old M.P. "Bob told me the very opposite."

"Who do you mean by 'Bob'?" demanded the young man.

"Why, Lord Salisbury, of course," was the retort. That anybody should have dared to call the Prime Minister "Bob" was as impossible as that the novice should have called the Leader of the House "Arthur" to his face; so the reprimand was complete.

No; it never occurred to anybody to take liberties with Lord Salisbury, any more than it would have occurred to him to "bluff" them. Once, indeed, the private secretaries' room at the Foreign Office was thrown into a ferment of indignation

when Li Hung Chang—the octogenarian tyrant-
ruler of China—entered the Secretary of State's
room for an interview, followed by a pipe-filling
menial and his cluster of little opium pipes. Now
Lord Salisbury had a well-known horror of tobacco,
whose fumes made him feel very uncomfortable;
moreover we were told that this strange procedure
on the part of the illustrious Chinese plenipotentiary
was in the nature of a " try-on." On the following
day, therefore, the Envoy was duly received to continue the conversation; but, somehow or another,
I contrived that the pipe-filler (who had arrived in
another carriage) should get lost in the passages of
the Foreign Office, and thus the two great men concluded their discussion without further inconven-
ience to the British Prime Minister.

Lord Salisbury at Hatfield was, to all except his
family, the same strong cloistered Personage that
he was in London. We saw very little of him except
at meals, unless we were sent for on business; then
he was generally to be found sitting at his table in
a pepper-and-salt country suit with a rug thrown
over his knees, in an over-heated atmosphere. He
always seemed to be working on foreign affairs in
his study, if he was not closeted in what Lord
Randolph Churchill once irreverently called " that
damned laboratory of his," where he indulged in
his only hobby of chemistry. It was rare, if my
memory serves me, to meet him out-of-doors; his

only forms of exercise were pounding along the park paths of Hatfield on a prehistoric tricycle or going for short but perilous expeditions on a very elementary motor-car driven, I think, by steam. Undoubtedly his strength was to sit still; to read and wrestle with his subject; to discuss it little, if at all, with anybody else; to come to his own conclusions and then to act upon them. "People" did not matter to him a bit; he neither recognised nor realised them, whether they were colleagues or casuals. I was at Hatfield when he walked up and down in the garden for half an hour with a delightful sporting peer under the impression that he was conversing with Field-Marshal Lord Roberts. It was then that I heard the story of his timid enquiry at a luncheon party as to the name of the gentleman sitting on his left. It turned out to be Mr. W. H. Smith, his principal colleague in Cabinet.* But nobody minded, whether colleague or subordinate; for the mere fact of being in his presence and hearing him talk was so tremendously worth while. He had in those latter days, what the author of *Eothen* called the majesty of true corpulence; a majesty that inspired reverence but not fear.

Life at Hatfield had a very patriarchal, simple character about it. There were the great Statesman and his brilliant wife; never so happy as when

* Once he said to me, "I really must learn to play bridge. If I don't, I shall never know Devonshire."

The Marquess of Salisbury with his Grandchildren

surrounded by their children and grandchildren
with whom, whatever their ages might be, the
Prime Minister used to talk as if they were his contemporaries and colleagues.* It was a very Liberty
Hall, where every member of the family did and
said what he liked, regardless of convention ; but
each of them realised that he (even the youngest
grandchild) had to take full responsibility for his
own deeds and words and abide by the consequences
of them—a thoroughly individualist training, which
might have been bad for most people but which
admirably suited the Cecils. For, although it never
taught them ' team-work, ' it established in every
one of them characteristics even more worth having ;
great self-reliance and an ascetic passion for high
principles for which they were equally ready to live
or die. This passion was surely inculcated through
a devout Christian training and by the splendid
example of their parents' spiritual lives. There were
family prayers in the house chapel every day, regular
Communions on Sunday morning at nine, and an
observance of the Sabbath which nowadays seems
almost impossible, but which was and still is at the
core of life at Hatfield. It invested the whole family
scene with the tranquil beauty of an English summer
evening, far apart from the turmoil and strife that
we associate with " the busy hum of men " ; and

* " He always talks to me as though I were an Ambassador, and
I _do_ like it," said one of his youthful sons about him.

it may easily account for the gentle confidence and
serene faith with which Lord Salisbury often took
arms for his country against a sea of troubles. More
often than not he ended them triumphantly ; but
then—" I hope there will be no trumpeting about
it." For he was a pacifist at heart, in the best sense
of the word, a man who hated war, guarded against
it, made " graceful concessions " to avoid it ; like
his ancestor, the Burleigh of Queen Elizabeth, he
was exceedingly cautious in his conduct of foreign
affairs. In this atmosphere of mental energy and
spiritual calm he directed the fortunes of our
Empire at home and abroad, exercising a restraining
influence upon a variety of destructive forces whose
power for evil lay pinioned until he died. How
often, by an impulsive misinterpretation of a provocative act or speech, he might have plunged our
country into a welter of blood and tears ! Instead
of which, he had the genius to know bluff from
business, and to differentiate truly between the
howlings of " public opinion " and the still small
voice of a nation, and so to save us from internal
disruption and from foreign war. I remember, in
this connection, a New Year party at Hatfield soon
after the Jameson Raid into the Transvaal—a huge
banquet, at which Princess Christian was present.
It was a brilliant scene, a splendid, old-fashioned
Yule-tide festival. About the middle of dinner a
footman brought an 'urgent' Foreign Office box,

containing a despatch, to Lord Salisbury, who
unlocked it and read the contents. He apologised
to the Princess, who said she hoped that it brought
no disagreeable news.

"No," said the Foreign Secretary; "not very.
It is only to tell me that the Germans have sent
two men of war into Delagoa Bay."

One can imagine how a novelist might have
dealt with the situation. He would have depicted
an embarrassed silence, then general consternation,
then the incontinent break-up of the feast; the
ordering of a special train for London, and the
hurried departure of the Secretary of State. Instead
of which Lord Salisbury quietly re-locked the box
and said casually to Her Royal Highness, with a
shrug of his massive shoulders, "What cheek,
Madam, what cheek!"; and the banquet went
blithely on.

"I hope you will not be laid up with 'Jingo-
fever' on your return from your tour": so he
wrote to me, in giving me leave to absent myself
for some months from the Foreign Office in order
to make a long journey in the East. That particular
quality or attribute of patriotism was most dis-
tasteful to him; he combatted it in public and in
private whenever he got the chance, usually with
a pointed phrase that pricked the soaring balloon
and let out the gas. For his whole conception of
policy and public duty was something like this:

it was best for the peace and progress of the world that those responsible for its governance should accept their heavy burden, strong in their belief in Divine guidance and fortified by their intensive training in public affairs ; that they should realise that they are called upon to control and lead the people, who would otherwise be led by impulse or emotion ; that it is often wiser in a leader to do nothing than to risk a false step which might lead to disaster ; that the conservative habit of reflection before great political changes, and of weighing the advantage against the disadvantage of change in the balance of past experience, is no bar to progressive legislation if the scales show that the proposed new measures are for the advancement of the people.

*" *Sero sed serio* " is the motto of the Cecil family. It is also the expression of an important quality in the character of the people of England.

* The late Harry Cust's ' free ' translation of this motto was " Late but Hungry."

LORD ROSEBERY
1847–1929

I HAVE often wondered whether my life would
have been greatly changed, and in what direction,
if I had accepted Lord Rosebery's suggestion that
I should become private secretary to Lady Rosebery
—an invitation conveyed to me by the late Lord
Esher in the year 1888, very soon after I had left
Oxford. I should, at any rate, have had a rather
earlier opportunity of enjoying the friendship of
Lord Rosebery, whose unfailing kindness to me
I can never forget. It began very shortly after
his wife's death in 1890, when I was an attaché
at the British Embassy in Berlin, and it only
ended when he died.

To us, the young men of that day who had
aspirations towards Parliament and ambition for
public service, Lord Rosebery was the *beau idéal*,
whether we were Liberals or Conservatives. To
us he seemed to have all that made life worth
living. The world was his oyster; the ball was at
his feet; in everything that we cared about he
was *facile princeps*. He was so clever that he could
afford to decline office under Mr. Gladstone in
the 1880 Parliament; and yet, only ten years

afterwards, his name was on every man's lips as
the G.O.M.'s probable successor to the leadership
of the Liberal party. He was a good, all-round
sportsman, with a first-rate racing stable ; he took
an interest in all games—except in first-class
cricket, which he once declared to me to be the
only cure he knew for insomnia ; he loved the
world's best things, good food and wine, art and
books ; he was an acknowledged leader of society,
with that genius for " mixing " which not only
caused him to be elected a member of the first
London County Council but also to become its
first Chairman in ·889. Everybody, east and west
of Piccadilly Circus, knew him by sight ; genial,
good-looking and beautifully turned-out. His past
speeches were admired, his future speeches were
eagerly looked forward to ; his *bons-mots* in conversation were boomed round the London that
had its centre in Berkeley Square. Men of my age
will probably realise why, although we admired
him, we were rather shy of him. We, with our
limited intelligences, could not understand why he
was a Liberal ; he seemed to be the repository of
all the attributes which the Liberals of that day
considered suspect, and to share but few of their
principles. And he cultivated, exclusively for the
benefit of his colleagues and of Society (with a
large S.), a Sphinx-like attitude, a faintly sarcastic
tone, and a gloomy manner which he could put

on or off at will. Perhaps we were even a little afraid of him—or we would have been, but for his attractive and disarming smile which immediately consoled after some sardonic observation had made us feel uncomfortable. That was his favourite form of chaff; but woe betide the man of any age who tried to use the same weapon against him. He did not suffer chaff gladly. Indeed, a hyper-sensitiveness to criticism of any kind was a striking trait—may I say a weakness?—in a character which fortune had otherwise fashioned to play a leading part in public affairs. And it seemed to grow with his growth, until it preyed upon him to an extent which may have been partly responsible for that insomnia which tormented him so sorely during and after the days of his Premiership.

But, when one got behind all that, one found in the real Lord Rosebery a most lovable and considerate personality, too introspective to be simple, but ardently sincere. One discovered that his cynicism was only a mask, often to hide a curious reserve that was in him, but that his affections were deep and real. Such were his feelings, for example, toward his political father and leader, Mr. Gladstone, as well as to his friend and disciple Sir Edward Grey, to Hew Dalrymple and to Ronald Munro-Ferguson, now Lord Novar, who should have been his Boswell. But Lord Rosebery

c

never carried his heart upon his sleeve " for daws
to peck at " ; those who needed it knew that they
would find it in the right place. For he was an
all-weather friend, in sickness and in health, to
the poor and to the rich, to the old and to the
young, perhaps especially to the young, with whom
he had so much in common. He seemed to take
a particular joy in making himself felt as a real
human being among all classes of his fellow countrymen ; his letters of condolence or congratulation,
written in his own hand to some of the humblest
of them, are as eloquent as the greatest of his
speeches.

Lord Rosebery was at his best in small parties
of his friends, for, as I have said, he was very
sensitive to atmosphere. I particularly remember
one such gathering, at Walmer Castle, on the
English Channel, when Lord Dufferin was Lord
Warden ; the other guests were Sir Arthur Nicolson
(the late Lord Carnock) and Sir Donald Mackenzie
Wallace. It was a revelation to me to sit with
those men on the battlements of that old Cinque
Port fortress and to hear them discussing, late into
the starry summer night, what might have happened
to England if Napoleon had ever set out upon his
famous expedition of invasion from those shores
whose distant lights we could see twinkling across
the Channel. In such a scene the artist Rosebery
soared high above the level even of his brilliant

companions. His strong dramatic instinct, his deep knowledge of the period, the magic of his voice—all of these, like the several stops of an organ, were combined under his hand to play us an historic symphony of enduring worth. The following afternoon we went for a sail on a choppy sea, but the conversation never flagged and I felt transported back into the early years of the nineteenth century, watching for the first signs of a hostile movement from the shores of France.

But that evening the scene changed ; after dinner we fell to talk of lighter things, led by Lord Dufferin's humour and Lord Rosebery's wit. The former, who was then our Ambassador in Paris, told us of his first official visit to the wives of the French Ministers. He had spoken to them of his delight at being in Paris, and at sleeping at our Embassy in the bed of " *la belle Pauline* " ; meaning, of course, Princess Pauline Borghese, to whom the house had formerly belonged. Then he described the suspicious silence which followed that harmless observation—" As though," he said, " I had boasted of sleeping in the bed of ' *la belle Siffleuse*,' " who was one of the music-hall celebrities of that day. And as the conversation ran on, Lord Dufferin mentioned that he had lately met an old friend of his, a titled lady who, through some misfortune, had undergone a short term of imprisonment. " I am now a perfect ruin," she moaned to Lord D., who confessed himself at a loss for an adequately sympathetic rejoinder. Then Lord R. : " I think I should have answered : ' So is the Colosseum.' "

As a host, Lord Rosebery was incomparable ; and I have no social recollections more agreeable than those of my visits to him in England and Scotland. He affected not to care very much about Mentmore, with its priceless collections of French furniture and *objets d'art*, and I often heard him say that he envied the simplicity of his lodge-keepers' cottages. He declared that he could never sit with ease upon a French chair ; which gives point to the story that, on one of his early visits to the Rothschild palace, he was discovered by his host in one of the drawing-rooms, reclining in a tin hip-bath (which he had brought down from his bedroom) wrapped in an old plaid and reading a French novel. In this preference he was curiously like Lord Salisbury, who once commented to me, as he looked at a Louis XIV armchair in somebody's house, or it may have been at Hatfield : " The French must have had very peculiar figures in those days, or very curious ideas of comfort."

Dalmeny was certainly a more comfortable house than Mentmore ; it may be pure imagination which makes me think that Lord Rosebery was happier there than in England. Atmosphere again, perhaps ; for the people of Edinburgh idolised him, and he

THE EARL OF ROSEBERY

[Daily Mirror

was hypnotised by the romantic history and beauty of that ancient city, only half-an-hour distant from Dalmeny. It was his spiritual home; he loved the heart of Midlothian with the ardour of a devotee to whom every stone of it was a shrine. And it was charged with memories of his early political days, of Mr. Gladstone's famous Midlothian campaigns, and of some of his own notable oratorical successes, whether as statesman or citizen, not inferior to those of the Grand Old Man himself. Lord Rosebery was justly called "the Spokesman of the Empire"; nobody has taken his place. I can see him now, in one or other of the great halls in Edinburgh, thrilling vast audiences with his matchless voice, as in measured tones he declared a policy or denounced a sham; his hands clasping the lapels of his coat, his wide-open, expressionless eyes gazing over the heads of his hearers; or leaning his arms upon the balustrade of a platform and staring into the faces, almost into the hearts, of a breathless multitude. A consummate master of language and of rhetoric, of irony and humour, Lord Rosebery could evoke in an audience a response to his every mood; he would stand back and glare at them when they cheered; his eyes would open as though in grave reproof when they laughed; and after a glowing peroration this supreme artist would quietly resume his seat, amid tempestuous applause, and seemingly

enquire what all this stir was about. Somehow,
I always felt that he was more at home with, and
spoke better to, a popular or a literary audience
than he did to the House of Lords where, although
his matter was of equal quality and his skill in
debate was formidable, he seemed in later years
to be straining for effect, and at times to become
almost melodramatic—pitching his voice to a loud,
gloomy note, thumping the table, raising his hands
high above his head, and finding great difficulty
in bringing them down again with intent and grace.

But the House of Lords and Lord Rosebery's
oratory are a far cry from Dalmeny, and from his
delightful little castle of Barnbougle, which stands
a few hundred yards away in the park on the shores
of the Firth of Forth. Thither let us return and
see Lord Rosebery, writing, reading, annotating,
handling and arranging his books with the enthusiasm and the care of the true book-lover—the
fine flower of the "budding bibliomaniac," as
William Cory called him in his Eton days. In
this citadel of his solitude he is surrounded by a
splendid Scottish library of books, nearly all of
which he has read and enhanced by marginal com-
ments of his own. Here is one : having discovered
that a piratical volume entitled *Edinburgh in the
days of Sir Walter Scott* was largely indebted to
Cockburn's Memorials for its text, and remembering
that the famous Scottish judge of that name was

related to the well-known Edinburgh wine-mer-
chants of the same name, Lord Rosebery writes
" I prefer my Cockburn undiluted." And another
—this time written in the biography of a celebrated
Scottish author : at the end of volume I, " Unspeak-
ably tedious " ; and, on finishing the book, " Inex-
pressibly boring. Why ? " I have spent hours
in this delightful fastness turning over the treasures
that he has collected, admiring his relics of Napoleon
and his portraits of celebrities so long as day-
light lasted ; and, when evening came, I retain
vivid recollections of tête-à-tête dinners, consisting
of grilled herrings, roast grouse and wonderful
claret, of listening to reminiscences and anecdotes
generously given from the store-house of a marvellous memory, and moonlight drives in a victoria
before retiring to bed.

One could almost feel that the various features
of Lord Rosebery's character were reproduced in
the houses that he inhabited and in their surroundings : at Mentmore the English squire and
his broad acres of agricultural land ; at Dalmeny
and Barnbougle the library man among his books,
breathing the air of Scottish romance which
permeated him through and through ; on the moors
at Rosebery the true sportsman and lover of nature,
keener about the quality than the quantity of the
game that he kills ; in Berkeley Square we find
the man of public affairs, the Prime Minister at

the centre of the political and social life of the
capital of the Empire; at the Durdans, the statesman *in villegiatura* and the patron of the Turf,
breeding, training and racing his horses in the
grand manner of the eighteenth century, and enter-
taining friends of every nationality at his lavish
board.

At the beginning of this century, thirty years
ago, five of us young Conservative M.P.'s formed
a small dining club, which Lord Salisbury nicknamed the "Hughligans" after his son Lord Hugh
Cecil; the other members being the late Lord
Percy, Winston Churchill, Arthur Stanley and
myself—hence the name of "Malcolmtents" by
which we were known to others. These two
soubriquets will indicate that we were, or thought
ourselves, an intrepid band of free lances who
charged against friend or foe with equal impartiality
and zest. Our manœuvres attracted the amused
interest of Lord Rosebery, with whom we spent
many a delightful week-end and discussed the
future of the Empire with grave irresponsibility.
His spell lay fast over us youthful politicians (he
was very happy in the society of those who admired
him) taking us into his confidence—not, perhaps,
very deeply—with a charm which was extremely
flattering to our aspiring souls. He taught us
many valuable things by precept, though not very
much by his example. Indeed, from time to time,

we parted from him with a sense of melancholy, feeling what a marvellous " might-have-been " he was—how nearly Bolingbroke, how nearly Pitt. " He longs for the palm without the dust," wrote his Eton tutor ; " how I wish I could get that lad to work." As it was in the beginning . . . so he continued ; like many a young man born with the proverbial silver spoon in his mouth —the only difference being that Lord Rosebery was born with a golden tea-set complete in his— his good was the enemy of his best, and his effort-less and varied gifts had to do duty for the drudgery that he would never face. School and college alike failed to discipline him ; he brought himself up, and he let himself down. One gift was denied him, the power of team-work. He was his own Minister of all the talents ; he was his own and only Privy Counsellor, and he was often badly advised. It is a curious fact that this prince of " good mixers " never seemed at home with his Cabinet colleagues. Of one of them he said to me, " How can I make a pet of a panther ? " ; of another, " His mind is so untidy that he is as likely to bring his washing-bill out of his pocket as the Memorandum which the Cabinet is waiting to discuss ; " and of a third (though this was told me long ago by somebody else) I must repeat the following anecdote. Mr. X., as we will call him, was a man whose brain was as acute as his appearance was undistinguished; this latter quality led him on one occasion to be ushered into the servants' quarters in a country house to which he had been invited, a misfortune which had been reported to Lord Rosebery. A year or two later Mr. X., now a Cabinet Minister, was talking, unguardedly and inaccurately apparently, about the domestic delinquencies of King Louis XV and his Court, until Lord Rosebery brought the conversation to an abrupt close by saying, " If X. knew as much about the halls of Versailles as he knows about the servants' hall at Castle Z. . . . he would not talk like that."

It was this tragic incompatibility of temper between him and those intimates with whom he found himself politically united, added to his inability to disguise his feelings, which robbed his Premiership of the distinction which should have adorned it, and which led him to plough his " lonely furrow " at an age when his splendid gifts should have been consecrated to the service of the Empire that he loved so well. Let those who would understand what was passing through Lord Rosebery's mind between, say, 1893 and 1896, remember first his dictum : " There are two supreme pleasures in life ; one is ideal, the other real. The ideal is when a man receives the Seals of Office from his Sovereign. The real pleasure comes when he hands them back." And then let the

student of this elusive character turn to his mono-
graph on William Pitt, and read his account of
the ill-feeling between Fox and Shelburne :

" It does not signify which of the two was to
blame for this mutual mistrust ; that it existed
is sufficient. It would be too much to maintain
that all the members of a Cabinet should feel
an implicit confidence in each other; humanity
—least of all political humanity—could not
stand so severe a test. But between a Prime
Minister in the House of Lords and the Leader
of the House of Commons such a confidence
is indispensable. . . . The voice of Jacob and
the hands of Esau may effect a successful
imposture but can hardly constitute a durable
administration."

Alter the names from Shelburne and Fox to
those of Rosebery and Harcourt, and no other
change in the above quotation is necessary to
describe the relationship between the Prime Minister
and his first lieutenant in 1894.

Let me end on a happier note. Mr. Goldwin
Smith once described the subject of this paper as
a revolving light, now flashing brilliantly, now
lost in deepest darkness, whilst the mariners watch
out anxiously for the next coruscation. That was
our attitude, an attitude of great expectations,

when Lord Rosebery practically abandoned politics but issued pretty frequently from his tent to address the world on Empire, historical or literary subjects. Such occasions were coruscations, indeed, and well worth waiting for. These will remain to cheer and inspire us long after we have (perhaps imprudently) forgotten his latest gloomy vaticinations delivered to the House of Lords ; they will serve to remind us of one of the most polished orators as well as of one of the most brilliant critics and many-sided personalities of the past fifty years.

* LORD BALFOUR

1848–1930

To the present generation of readers who may be called upon to study the biographies of great personalities of the present century, to which my volume of sketches is a kind of illustrated handbook, the subject of this chapter has always been Lord Balfour, though for the previous fifty years he was known to the world of politics and philosophy and London society as Mr. Balfour or as A.J.B.

For forty years I knew him fairly intimately, as a friend, a political follower and as his private secretary. But in these pages my principal concern with him is as a public man whose name will for long years to come be connected with many aspects of the fortunes of our country during the last half century of its history. Being surrounded, on both sides of his family and by marriages therein, by relatives immersed in public affairs, he could hardly escape the tyranny of environment or fail to follow in their footsteps. Nor, indeed, did he so fail, although at Cambridge University, of which he died the Chancellor, he showed little instinct or aptitude for a public career. He often

* Created Earl of Balfour, 1922.

said that, had circumstances permitted, he would have liked to devote himself to science; but I was recently told by one of his sisters that many years ago he had confided in her that he now had no regrets on this score, since he "never would have had patience enough to be a man of science, waiting for the results of experiments." So, possibly for that reason, science receded into the background as a profession, though it remained well to the fore as a secondary interest for him, and philosophy took its place. Doubtful once more as to his final calling, he consulted his brother-in-law, Professor Henry Sidgwick, upon whose judgment he set the highest value. The result of this consultation was that, either by direct advice or by suggestion, Mr. Balfour convinced himself that he should enter the political arena, although he never abandoned his philosophical way of looking at every problem presented to him. Balfour's early years in Parliament were marred by uncertainty of health which prevented him from taking any strenuous or distinguished part in the life of the House of Commons. He served his uncle fitfully at the Foreign Office during Mr. Disraeli's last administration; he travelled extensively and attended the Berlin Congress as private secretary to Lord Salisbury. All this time his mind was hard at work and his body was growing into its proper strength. Then came the days of the

Fourth Party; with it the name of Balfour became closely associated, and, through assiduous practice in debate, he laid the foundations of his future success. The languid-looking student, half philosopher and half artist, quickly developed into the alert and dexterous dialectician, the practised debater, the courageous statesman whose brilliant term of office as Chief Secretary for Ireland qualified him for the highest posts in the gift of the Crown. And thus it came about that, twenty-five years or so after his first election to Parliament, A.J.B. was First Lord of the Treasury and leader of his party in the House of Commons, which latter office he held continuously until he resigned it in 1911. During that long period his responsibilities were great and continuous, but they never overtaxed his courage or his intellectual powers. His physical health, however, was still a pre-occupation, and there were times when his friends doubted how long he could endure continual attacks of influenza and lesser ailments without giving in. The signs of his physical frailty were familiar to all his fellow-members; his trick of leaning so far back on the Front Bench that he seemed to be reclining on his shoulder-blades, with his long legs resting on the table in front of him; and his later habit of sniffing from a little tube some mixture which his doctor had given him to clear his nasal passages and give resonance to his voice

—this was a movement which was the invariable preface to his rising, and it was constantly repeated all through his speech. But it was a case of the struggle for supremacy between mind and body ; as he grew older he certainly became far stronger, his absences from the House on account of illness were less frequent, and, as we all know, some of his best and most important work for the country was done during the last ten years of his long life.

I have written elsewhere* of his personal charm and popularity alike among friends and foes in Parliament. I do not suppose that he was conscious of possessing these rare attractions, any more than he appreciated how much his friendship meant to those who enjoyed it. If he had realised that, I know that he would have shown it in some other way (I cannot express it in words) than by appearing to offer to everybody the same meed of good companionship. Perhaps that is what made some people think him ungrateful—the last fault of which he could be accused. But it never crossed his mind, humble as it was in some things, that men or women thought of him more or were ready to give him more than was the due portion of their other friends. And if this was a short-coming, he never improved on it ; for those whom it chafed forgot and forgave it as soon as they saw him again. In friendship, as in everything

* *Lord Balfour : a Memory*, by Sir Ian Malcolm (Macmillan), 1930.

else, he was utterly sincere; he may now and
then have disguised what he felt, but he never
affected a sentiment or a belief that he did not
feel. It was just the genuineness of him that made
the man so beloved; his genuine gladness to see
old friends and to make new ones; his genuine
interest in the lives and occupations of all around
him; his genuine preferences and dislikes for some
people and some things—all of which he showed
in language and manner peculiarly his own. So,
let no one think that I am describing him as lacking
in heart because he did not disclose it to all and
sundry. It was not so; there were crises in the
lives of a few of his closest friends when his deep
and abundant sympathy pervaded and consoled
them; there were stark moments in his own life
when his heart was sore unto death.

Of course he had some supporters who criticised
his policy from time to time, and opponents who
detested it all the time; but there were none,
not even among the Irish, who did not feel that
their duty of opposition would have been far
easier if the object of their hostility had been of
coarser fibre than A.J.B. They admired his fair-
ness in debate, his readiness in reply, his humour,
and his courage in never failing to give battle where
a question could be fought out squarely on the
floor of the House. What the Nationalists did
not like was his disdain of invective and vitu-

D

peration when aimed at him. Either he appeared
not to hear it, as he leaned back negligently in
his seat, or, if it was necessary for him to follow,
he addressed the House apparently in complete
ignorance that any personal attack had been made
upon him. This form of negative riposte was so
deadly that, in the course of two or three years,
the attacks ceased and more serious argument was
substituted for them. Such was the Arthur
Balfour of the House of Commons, whether in
or out of office; brilliant, courteous, serene.
Then there were other A.J.B.'s, combining all
these qualities with others : the temperament, for
example, that could not tolerate chicane or injustice
and lashed them with calculated phrases that cut
like a diamond. And there were people who
failed at first to grasp the fact that under that
external suavity there lay, for essentials, an adamantine quality of determination. The English never
realised this until it was too late. But the Irish
did at the beginning of his career ; so did Monsieur
Clemenceau during the Peace Conference in Paris.
He called A.J.B. " the Richelieu of the Congress :
the most courteous and the most adamantine of
men." More than any other, it was this latter
quality which compelled him to remain Prime
Minister during the troublous years of 1904–5
whilst his colleagues were resigning all around him.
He was sincerely anxious, judging from the imme-

LORD BALFOUR
in Paris

diate past, as to what the foreign policy of a
Liberal administration under Campbell-Bannerman
might be ; and he was determined that the recently-
sown seeds of alliance with Japan and with France
should have time to take root and grow without
risk of disturbance. He was determined also
that, before a professedly " pacifist " Government
succeeded the Unionists, the British Army should
be equipped with the new rifle which would put
it on an equality in that respect with the greater
armies on the Continent. The English did not
understand him : there were masses of them who
professed to think that, all through the strife of
tariffs, he was clinging to office to serve some
ulterior and obscure ambition of his own. In
the fullness of time this quality of determination
will be made clear in the light of hitherto unpub-
lished papers, which will do much to dispel the
doubts that were inevitably felt as to the wisdom
or unwisdom of his policy during those two
eventful years.

And in summing up his character we must not
forget the deep spiritual thinker who could write
books like *The Foundations of Belief*, or give such
addresses as the Gifford Lectures at Glasgow
University : nor the artist with his love of pictures
and of classical music, who could discuss string
quartets with Joachim ; Bach's or Handel's ora-
torios with Hubert Parry ; or painting with Burne-

Jones. Of his love of literature whole chapters might be written : Arthur Balfour's appetite for refreshing his soul from the fountains of old authors and for keeping abreast with the spirit of the new age was only equalled by his power of assimilating and thriving upon all that he read. His mind was so constructed that he could be temporarily engrossed in three or four books at the same time ; books so widely divergent in purpose, for instance, as a work on philosophy, a treatise on military history, and the latest detective story. Indeed, on one occasion he publicly acknowledged

" the advantages of an omnivorous, universal and insatiable curiosity to know everything that can be known. . . . It is a pleasure that lasts longer than any other. It is an appetite not followed by satiety, which is independent of changes and circumstances, or of the love or dislike of your fellow-men."

And his interest in scientific subjects was no less unflagging. Has he not told us that " Newton was perhaps the greatest man the world has ever seen " ; by that eulogy he disclosed something more of his innermost self, and he opened the door of his mind a little wider when he declared: " I would rather be known as having added something to our knowledge of truth and nature than for anything else I could imagine." I am not competent to go further into this side of A.J.B.'s character, an aspect which is charmingly and faithfully developed by his nephew, Lord Rayleigh, in his Memoir on *Lord Balfour and his Relation to Science.*

Finally the sporting A.J.B. : the ardent stalker and rifle shot, the University representative at real tennis, the bicyclist, the devotee of golf, and the persistent player of lawn-tennis until he was nearly eighty years old ; the delightful companion of old and young, with his keen interest in every old treasure and every new invention or book ; talking to all comers seriously or fancifully, as suited the spirit of the moment, and always listening as brilliantly as he talked.

What wonder that such a man, possessed of the rare combination of all these gifts, made himself felt and loved, without an effort, wherever he went. This was especially noticeable from the close of the War and for ten years onward, when his official duties led him for the first time into foreign lands. When he first went to America in 1917 he took the States by storm. Overworked as he was with new duties, he found time to see and talk to everybody upon the subjects that they wanted to hear about. He had secret conferences with President Wilson, larger ones with trades unions and experts, meetings with the Jews and with the Irish and

Labour parties, luncheons and dinners and receptions with all and sundry. Washington and New York and Richmond (Virginia) tried to outrival one another in doing honour to their new and illustrious guest, who went through the fatigues of each recurring day with the zest and enjoyment of a man of forty ; and when it was all over, after five strenuous weeks, the leave-takings and the farewells were touching in their reciprocal sincerity. So it was in France during the Peace Conference ; there was, by common consent, no man at that unwieldy congress of unnumbered nations who could, like him, compose grave difficulties, suggest compromises, find solutions for apparently insoluble problems and promote harmony among rivals. Then came Geneva and the League of Nations, with its legacies of tasks unfulfilled at Paris ; there again the gracious and elegant figure moved serenely through a labyrinth of complications with confidence, as though he were saying " Have patience ; we will find a way." And then to America once more for the Washington Conference on armaments and to reap further successes ; to Jerusalem and Syria on a journey of encouragement to Zionists, and back again to his home land for the Imperial Conference and the duties connected with his position as Lord President of the Council. At last, at the age of eighty-two, strength failed him, and he died as serenely as he had lived.

I have tried, in this rapid outline of A.J.B.'s varied and important activities, to give to his successors a rough sketch of a great man ; and, particularly, to show them by his example that force of mind and character can overcome the weakness of the flesh by the absorption of self in the execution of public duty. Also to suggest that, even in these days of haste and pressure, the man serene and cultured and patient can still be of immense service to the State.

SIR HENRY CAMPBELL-BANNERMAN
1836–1908

THERE are some things lying patent to the eye which nobody sees. For instance: in the year of grace 1895 nobody saw that C.-B. was bound, sooner or later, to lead the Liberal party and ultimately to become Prime Minister of England. On the contrary: nobody paid much attention to the genial, stout, smiling little man buttoned into a tight frock-coat, who appeared to be friends with everybody and to take but a languid or spasmodic interest in parliamentary affairs. I do not know why that was, for I was a new-comer to Westminster in that year. After all, he had been in Liberal Governments for over twenty years: at the War Office, at the Admiralty, as Chief Secretary for Ireland, and he had just recently served in Lord Rosebery's Cabinet. He had even let it be known that he would like to be chosen Speaker of the House of Commons, an ambition which was only thwarted by his colleagues who said they could not spare him from the Front Bench, whether in Government or in Opposition. Such was his "previous history": yet, at the moment, he did not count; and I daresay he did not want to. But as time went on, and as the rift between the Rosebery and the Harcourt factions grew wider and deeper, C.-B. was about the only man on the Opposition benches who could hold out a friendly hand from the main stream of Liberalism to the laird of Dalmeny in his furrow on the one bank and to the squire of Malwood on his high horse on the other. But for his efforts, soothing and unobtrusive, the plight of his party would have been even worse than it was ; the party recognised the fact and promoted him to the distinction of being henceforth known *urbi et orbi* as " C.-B."—a sure proof of popularity. So, when Sir William Harcourt and John Morley surrendered their joint leadership of the Liberals in 1898, C.-B. slipped quite naturally into the succession. As a good party man he was universally known and liked ; as a leader he was an unknown quantity. At that time the general impression was that he had been an able administrator, but that he was indolent ; fond of long holidays on the Continent, ill-disposed for the rough and tumble of parliamentary warfare, and far more conversant with French yellow-backed novels than with British Blue-books. The only certain factor in his " make-up " was all to his credit : he was slow but sure in forming his opinion upon any subject ; but, once formed, he let that opinion be known to friend and foe, and he never changed it. So

that people knew where they were with " C.-B."
Had he not said, with characteristic candour, in
his first election address :

> " If you wish to draw any augury from my
> close connection with my father, Sir James
> Campbell, then I would have you believe that
> possibly the staunchness may run in the blood,
> that I may inherit his tenacity without his prin-
> ciples, and that as my father, through a long
> life, through good report and evil report, in
> fair weather and foul, has stuck to his Tory
> party, so his son, in like manner, will stick to
> his."

No Rembrandt or Raeburn could have portrayed
more faithfully than does that sentence the outstanding character of Campbell-Bannerman.   He
had courage and he had consistency ; he was also
said to have infinite powers of conciliation, which
he exercised with great effect when he became leader
of the Liberal party ; I never saw him even try to
conciliate his political opponents.

Such, then, was the man that the Liberals chose
to lead them out of the wilderness when Rosebery,
Harcourt and Morley had forsaken them and fled
to their respective tents.   It was no easy task for
any man, and well C.-B. knew it.   On the one side
of him he had Harcourt and Morley, the two

SIR HENRY CAMPBELL-BANNERMAN

ex-leaders of the party, not hostile but disgruntled ;
on the other side, Asquith and Edward Grey—
much younger men, of keener intellectual ability
than himself, both of whom had held high and
responsible office in Lord Rosebery's Government
three or four years ago, and both of them " Liberal-
Imperialists " to the core.   These, plus Mr. Haldane,
were his " flankers " : behind him, sawn and riven
asunder by utterly opposing principles, were the
remains of the great Liberal Party upon which he
had to rely to keep up a respectable appearance
of parliamentary opposition.   Poor man !

Then, to make confusion worse confounded,
came the Boer War ; when the " Rosebery-ites "
drifted even further apart from the Gladstonians
and gave Lord Salisbury's Government a general
support against " C.-B.," whose party was beaten
to its knees at the " Khaki Election " of 1900—
" *magni nominis umbra*."   But even with his decimated
legions and his unpopular cause of pro-Boerism,
C.-B. put up a brave and obstinate fight ; so much
must his opponents all admit, though we were
daily goaded into fury by his speeches, hated
his methods and loathed his " little England "
ideals.   But what a change came over this
nonchalant, easy-going, pleasure-loving Scot, once
he was in the saddle as leader of a forlorn
hope.   The man was transformed : he became
(apparently) short-tempered, even bad-tempered

at times; he shuffled on his feet, he tugged at
his collar, he shot out his under-lip, he spoke
violently from sheets of notes which contained
streams of invective and scorn and parliamentary
abuse, and he gave the utmost support to followers
like Lloyd George, Philip Stanhope and Labouchere
who were even more vituperative than himself.
In this fire of righteous indignation, as they conceived it, the new Radical party was born. And
C.-B. was its intrepid leader all through the Tariff
Reform fights which began as soon as the Boer
War was over; his was the personal attraction
which brought back Asquith and Haldane and
Grey with their adherents into his 'tabernacle' and
formed the serried phalanx that was to win the
battle for Free Trade at the General Election of
1906, with a majority which made one think that
the Liberals would be in power in England until
the Day of Judgment. How strange a transforma-
tion : of this man of parliamentary Peace seeking
in 1898 to gather up and frame together the frag-
ments of Mr. Gladstone's once great organisation
into the semblance of a party; then shattering it
by his own vehement anti-war policy; and finally
becoming the parliamentary genius who welded
together into a formidable fighting and victorious
army the scattered and disbanded troops who must
have thought that they had fought their last battle
for Liberalism in 1900. I have felt bound to

dwell on these early days because only those who lived through them and saw the change and development in C.-B.'s methods, if not in his character, can realise his rapid rise from the domesticated, hum-drum administrator, a politician *malgré lui*, to the triumphant Generalissimo of a consolidated Liberal army until the outbreak of another great war which shattered it once again.

It was not until he became Prime Minister in 1906 that " C.-B." began to take a prominent interest in Foreign Affairs from the political point of view. He had, from his youth up, travelled widely, was a sound classical scholar, had a competent knowledge of German, and spoke French with an accent and facility most unusual among Ministers of the British Crown. He was, therefore, quite at home in his new surroundings, which entailed meetings and conferences with distinguished foreigners with whom he was immediately at ease and could converse without the semblance of an effort. To him a public speech in French involved no strain of any kind ; I heard him make several of them, and shall never forget his allocution to the delegates of the Russian Parliament, I think in the Waterloo Chamber, when he closed his speech with the exclamation, startling from so staid an orator, " *La Duma est morte ; vive la Duma* ". This was an electric shock, coming from the Prime Minister of a conservative country, only two days after the Czar had dismissed his parliament rather in the manner of a Stuart King. But it was a calculated shock, and it had its effect in the same way that his violent explosion of " Enough of this foolery ! " had on another occasion. These outbursts, however, were very rare after C.-B. became Premier ; indeed, he seemed from that time to affect the character of a conciliator; of a man of business who would rather deal than fight, and who was anxious to show that the re-constructed Liberal party could transact the country's business quite as expeditiously and efficiently as its predecessors. This could only be achieved by pacific rather than by shock tactics, for his programme (like all Liberal programmes) was overloaded, and his team had not had sufficient time to cement themselves into a homogeneous whole. He had ahead of him an Education Bill for England, land legislation, the pacification of South Africa, a Devolution Bill for Ireland, a Licensing Bill and every prospect of an imminent quarrel with the House of Lords. These were but a few of the salient features, explicit or implied, in his first King's Speech. But patience and " pawkiness " won through in the long run, and even his most doughty opponents had to admit that he managed the House and the party and the business with considerable skill in the face of a determined though attenuated Conservative Opposition. And all this he achieved when sorely beset by anxiety on account of Lady Campbell-Bannerman's illness, which involved his constant absences from the House of Commons in order to be in attendance at her bedside in London, Paris or Marienbad, a duty from which no public obligations could swerve him and which only ended with the death of his life-long companion and counsellor in August 1906. This sad stern decree of Providence seemed only to steel his determination to see his political programme through, a course which he pursued for two long years with a broken heart and failing health, earning the sympathy and respect of even the keenest of his political opponents for the courage and thorough-bred tenacity with which he ran his course. Everything possible was done to lighten the burden of his public duties; His Majesty King Edward (to whom in his last years he became devotedly attached) setting an example in this respect which was gladly followed by all his colleagues. At last he offered his resignation to his Sovereign; and within a fortnight he was gathered to his fathers, just forty years after he had entered the House of Commons.

It is not for me to judge whether history will ultimately grade C.-B. as a Prime Minister of the first or of lesser rank. But of this I am sure; that he came from the same rock out of which great Prime Ministers, perhaps with happier opportunities, are hewn. He had conviction and courage; he had patience and perseverance, he had kindliness, dignity and humour. And this is the record of one who sincerely disapproved of nearly everything that C.-B. did or said publicly during the thirteen eventful years that they were fellow-members of the House together, of one who now regrets that he could not see the quality of the gold in the man's character through the flames of controversy which were proving it; of one, nevertheless, who gladly subscribes to the words uttered by General Smuts in South Africa in 1917:

"I hope when you draw up a calendar of empire-builders, you will not forget the name of Campbell-Bannerman, a wise man with profound feeling and profound political instinct who achieved one of the wisest political settlements in the history of this country."

*LORD OXFORD AND ASQUITH

1852–1928

MR. ASQUITH, as I prefer to remember him, belonged to the race of " Ironsides " ; a new type on the list of Prime Ministers of England, and one admirably fitted to carry out the inflexible and radical programme to which the Liberal party set its seal on returning to power in 1906 after nearly twenty years of Conservative government. And he was a new type of leader for the Liberals of that day, whose pent-up and generous enthusiasms were inclined to outrun the pace of political discretion and of parliamentary possibility.

Looking back on those times of a generation ago, I do not think that any of us then realised the run of luck which favoured our opponents in 1906, united them and provided them with exactly the generals that they needed. I do not say or think that there was any luck in the result of the General Election at the end of 1905 which gave them a majority of overwhelming proportions at a time when their domestic differences made them anything but a happy family. But I do think that it was a piece of rare good fortune for them to

* Created Earl of Oxford and Asquith, 1925.

have ready to hand a man of the type of Campbell-
Bannerman, whose temperament and example
were supremely suited to healing dissensions,
stifling personal ambitions, allaying suspicions,
and, in a word, making a formidable team out of
a fissiparous and unwilling majority. Then,
following on that achievement (which, perhaps,
cost him his life), were they not fortunate again
in securing Mr. Asquith as his successor, a man
of quite different calibre and character, whose
industry, experience and stalwart reputation
were precisely the qualities necessary to inspire
that team to reach the goal of their political
desire ?

My acquaintance with Mr. Asquith dates back
to the 1895 Parliament, when he and Sir Edward
Grey were the acknowledged " coming men " on
the Opposition Front Bench, the rising hopes of
those *frondeurs* who looked askance at anything
resembling an " old gang." Both of them had
won their spurs at Balliol and in the House of
Commons. Asquith had already been Home
Secretary (under Mr. Gladstone and Lord Rosebery)
and Sir Edward had been Under-Secretary at the
Foreign Office ; both had done remarkably fine
work. It required little perspicacity to prophesy
that these two men were destined, after the turn
of the tide, to take very high place in the councils
of the nation. And so we young men watched

them with interest across the floor of the House, and wondered when their chance would come.

Asquith was a very rare speaker in those days, but always well worth hearing or reading afterwards in Hansard. He was endowed with the gift of compression in an age of prolixity, which made his contributions welcome to those of a generation which (in its parliamentary youth at any rate) was more anxious to get on with business than to hear a Front Bench orator, on either side, " get off " a speech. But there is much more to be said about his House of Commons style; he and Mr. Chamberlain between them founded a new school of speaking at Westminster—a school not so remarkable for eloquence or enthusiasm as for condensation, cold logic and hard fact. That these qualities could be clothed in terse and beautiful English it was Mr. Asquith's privilege to prove. No Roman senator—and Asquith's clean-cut profile and his stately diction often reminded one of such a senator—could have surpassed in purity of language and perfection of form the best of his speeches. A Frenchman once said of him that he was the favourite political apostle of the business man; that his *imperiosa brevitas* appealed to the new House of Commons; *tout semblait préparé et voulu*. He called him *cet artiste austère*; a Master of Facts rather than of Arts, for whom philosophic argument had no attraction and who never disguised himself in the folds of an expert's gown.

Asquith once told an audience of old boys at the City of London School much the same thing. He said that there he had not only imbibed the ordinary lessons but had added to his studies " something actual and realistic." He had also, at that early age, a clear vision of what he might become in after life. It is related that, whilst a school-boy, he invited one of his teachers to examine him (out of school hours) in points of constitutional law and of parliamentary procedure. On being asked why he bothered his head about such things, he is said to have replied that he wished some day to be Prime Minister or Lord Chancellor of England.

At Balliol, as we all know, he had a brilliant career, and shone conspicuously in a constellation of distinguished contemporaries. He took a First Class degree, became President of the Union and was subsequently elected to a Fellowship of his old college ; with all these honours falling thick upon him he was called to the Bar and worked hard for his living. But it is by his performances in the Senate and not in the Law Courts that Asquith made the name by which he will be remembered. Indeed, it will always remain something of a mystery to me that his record as barrister is not a more brilliant one, endowed as he was with a brain which C.-B. once described as " a faultless piece of machinery ", that made him one of the intellectual masters of the House of Commons. Perhaps it may be that he just lacked something of the fire of imagination, the self-revealing power, which brings conviction to the mind of a jury; that, as someone wrote of him, " he requires more blood; iron he has in plenty and of excellent quality "; and that this deficiency, together with an economy of missionary fervour, explains the matter. But, however that may be, the loss to the law was a double gain to the legislature from the moment that he first sat upon a Front Bench and concentrated all his powers upon furthering the solution of industrial and labour problems. " It is a higher and a harder task to make than to take a city," he once observed in a speech; and thus we learn the trend of his political ambition in his earlier days, fortified as it was by personal knowledge and experience of the social conditions of life and industry in the North of England. To him might well be applied, at that time, the lines written in honour of an earlier race of reformers along the same lines :

> " He had stiff knees, the Puritan,
>   That were not made for bending ;
> The home-spun dignity of man
>   He thought was worth defending."

Of such stern unbending stuff was he made, this
" stocky " man of medium height, round-headed
and square-shouldered, who could fill the House
whenever he rose to attack or to dissect a Conservative policy with relentless criticism until he had
satisfied himself that nothing remained to be said
for it in defence. That he failed to satisfy his
opponents goes, of course, without saying in an
assembly where private judgment is often obscured
by party loyalty ; but it may perhaps be said that
he did not always completely satisfy his supporters,
to whom he brought little of the joy of battle,
so dear to the rank and file of every political party,
nor any of the fires of a consuming faith, but
only the calm contribution of a great intellect as
hard as flint and as cold as steel. He certainly
did not wear his heart upon his sleeve—an inconvenient place for the heart of any man in his position—but there was something of truth in the
observation of one of his most ardent followers,
that " Asquith's heart is concealed so deep down
in his pocket that we are inclined to doubt whether
he has one." This applied to his private relations
to his party no less than to his public utterances.
Someone wrote of him, about this time, that " he
meets the world in the office of his thoughts, not
in the parlour," and I believe that to have been
true. He was not a man with a nickname; he was
not the central figure of amusing anecdotes in

EARL OF OXFORD

the lobby or the smoking-room; he was a man
of massive simplicity (to use a description of him
by Mr. J. A. Spender)—a "sledge-hammer" as
C.-B. liked to call him—whose title to his party's
confidence rested upon his well-founded boast
that "he fought the Tories and not his fellow-
Liberals," upon his keen intellectual powers, and
upon his proven loyalty to his colleagues. That
confidence he had, and one felt it whenever he got
up to make a great speech or a difficult reply in
debate.

Asquith was very quiet, almost impassive, when
speaking in the House. He rose very quietly,
placed his notes on the box before him, surveyed
his audience rather benevolently for a moment,
gave a little hitch with his shoulders and then
began his speech in low and even tones. His
speeches never seemed to take much out of him;
for one thing they were never long and his gestures
were few and far between. I can only remember
three of them: a twitch at his collar, a spring
back from the table, and a blow from his right
fist upon the palm of his left hand when anxious
to make a very particular point. Occasionally,
like most men, he was roused or offended by some
interjection whilst he was speaking. Then he
flushed to the roots of his hair, threw back his
head, gave a slight sniff and dealt with the inter-
rupter as the occasion demanded. He was cer-

tainly the finest parliamentary orator of the classic
kind during my time in the House of Commons,
with a few insignificant mannerisms (such as his
love of antitheses and of jingling phrases) to
which we looked forward, and even counted at
times, but which never clouded the limpidity of
his language nor frayed the thread of his argument.
For illustration or flights of rhetorical imagination
he had little use; I never heard him indulge in a
prepared peroration. He did not lack humour in
private conversation, very far from it; but it did
not suit his parliamentary style, which is probably
the reason why he employed it so seldom. One
rather typical example of his lighter manner may
serve to remind others of it. One night, during
the Tariff Reform controversy, we were promised
a full-dress debate; but when it was opened neither
Mr. Balfour nor Mr. Chamberlain were in their
places, an opportunity which Asquith used for
remarking that this discussion was as vain as a
performance of Hamlet without the Prince of
Denmark or the Ghost, though he would not
presume to allocate the parts.

Such is my impression of this leading parliamentarian, this implacable Radical Prime Minister, up
to the conclusion of the great Constitutional fight
over the House of Lords. From that time onward,
as it seemed to me, he began to tire, to lose grip
a little, to drive the House of Commons (and, it

was said, the Cabinet also) with too light a rein.
The Ironside of a few years ago appeared to be
exchanging his armour of asceticism for a genial
and comfortable costume more attractive to
advancing years. The hard-working recluse, the
home-spun Puritan, appeared more frequently in
London society and mixed freely with those who
had congenial companionship to offer him. That
inflexible will seemed to soften and, on occasion,
to allow itself to be compelled along unwonted
paths by at least one colleague with driving power
and with ambition far superior to his own. Then
came the War, which exacted from every man
and woman in the realm the maximum of energy
which it was theirs to give, and from the Prime
Minister an almost super-human and inexhaustible
display of energy, will-power and decision. It
was after two years of unremitting labour in respect
of public affairs at home and abroad that Mr.
Asquith made way for another Premier, in obedience
to the prevailing sense of the country at that time.
The surrender must have been hard indeed after
all that he had won for his party, without a rival
near his throne during the past twenty years ;
but he made it, and retired with dignity to a seat
on the Opposition Front Bench, whence he gave
a general if critical support of the conduct of the
Great War, at the close of which he lost his seat
during the " Coupon " Election of 1918. He

remained, however, leader of the Liberal party, and was soon back (1920) in the House of Commons as Member for Paisley, where he remained until 1924 when he suffered defeat once more, and finally retired from the House in which he had been a leading personality and a commanding figure for forty years. In the following January, and to the satisfaction of all his friends, His Majesty conferred on Mr. Asquith—still leader of his party—the dignity of an Earldom with the title, which was more than a little criticised, of Earl of Oxford and Asquith, an honour which was soon to be followed by his becoming a Knight of the Garter. As with so many other great Commoners, he felt ill at ease in the atmosphere of the Lords, where he spoke seldom, but always with telling effect. His principal speech was on the General Strike in 1926, a pronouncement which—coupled with his correspondence with Mr. Lloyd George—led to his resignation of the leadership of the Liberal Party. This irrevocable decision was the cause of almost universal regret, and Mr. Baldwin expressed the feelings of the whole of the Unionist party when he wrote to him:

" Secure in the respect and affection of your friends, indeed of all Englishmen whose respect and affection are worth having, may you have as many years of peace and happy rest as you desire and not one more ! "

His last speech was made at York on October 19th, 1927, and in the February following, alas, that powerful voice was for ever stilled. And here is the fine testimony to his public character, spoken by his old colleague and Foreign Secretary, Lord Grey of Fallodon :

" He was willing that his own personality should be a shelter in adversity, but in fair weather he would stand aside lest he should cast a shadow on any colleague who was entitled to the light."

MR. BONAR LAW

1858–1923

THE rise of Bonar Law to parliamentary fame always
strikes me as the most meteoric achievement ever
performed at Westminster. Entering as a new
member during the Boer War in 1900, a Glasgow
iron-master with no political ancestry nor training
nor friends, he joined Mr. Balfour's Ministry in
1902, succeeded him as leader of the Unionist
party in 1911 and, about ten years afterwards,
became the Tory Prime Minister of England. This
surprised most people, but it surprised " Bonar "
least of all. He was a man of gentle and retiring
manners in private life, conscious (one would
have thought) of his political limitations and
without any strong ambition to shine in that
particular firmament. Such was the first impression
one got on seeing that neat, reserved, sad-looking
man, seeking his way about the House of Commons
and more generally finding it to the smoking-room
where the chess-boards were set out than to the
forum of debate. But the impression was an
entirely wrong one : for we had not reckoned
with, because we did not know, the stern characteristics of will and courage and decision which,

added to carefully-concealed but great ambition, had made him one of the most prominent and successful citizens of Glasgow.

We were not long, however, in finding out our mistake; it required exactly two speeches from him to convince us of it. One was on the Corn duties (at the outset of the Tariff controversy) and the other upon some complicated question in connection with coal. In those days Bonar always constructed and delivered his speeches in the same way—rather like a clever young don lecturing a class of undergraduates, his hands clasped behind his back, without a note to help him; terribly earnest and sincere, an unmodulated voice, a pronounced Doric accent, and rather clockwork gestures when, if ever, these were needed. There was no attempt at humour and very little imagination. Always suffused with an atmosphere of business philosophy, his speeches were closely packed with figures and facts so admirably arranged and so lucidly presented that they were easy for the non-expert to follow. I can only think of two other men who shared with Bonar Law this rare and attractive gift of making the involved appear intelligible to the lay mind by the process of effortless exposition—they were Mr. Alexander Ure (afterwards Lord Strathclyde) and Mr. Fletcher Moulton, who later became a Lord of Appeal. These speeches of Bonar were, as I have said,

delivered without a note; they were excogitated
in an arm-chair with a pipe, and learned *verbatim*
without a word being written down even in the
course of preparation. It might well be thought
that this somewhat rigid method would easily be
put out of gear by interruption, or by the necessity
of impromptu reply to a point raised by a previous
speaker. But, in the case of Bonar, this was not
so; he was so sure of his facts, so certain that
others must be wrong when they contradicted
him that, from the very outset, he found no difficulty in breaking the thread of his main argument
to dispose of an enemy in the gate, and in making
his telling reply appear to be of a part with his
prepared speech, which was then continued to its
conclusion.

These two speeches brought Bonar into Mr.
Balfour's Government in 1902 and everyone
approved the Prime Minister's choice. They also
justified Mr. Joseph Chamberlain in choosing him
for his first lieutenant in the Fiscal campaign which
was soon to be launched upon the country. Into
that campaign Bonar Law threw himself body and
soul; and, although a new-comer to Parliament,
he never ceased to attack the high priests of Free
Trade in their own sanctuary which they had been
guarding when he was a boy at school. It might
have been better for his training as the future
Prime Minister—a post which demands a modicum

of diplomacy in its occupant to ensure his success—
if Bonar's *fortiter in re* had included a touch of
the *suaviter in modo*. But this latter ingredient had
no part either in his intellectual or his forensic
make-up. Besides which, there is this to be said:
the tariff question, like religious questions and
Home Rule (which was very much mixed up with
religion) always appears to rouse all parties in
the House of Commons to a pitch of unbalanced
excitement and of quite inexcusable verbal license.
Those who are moved by these particular subjects
are deeply moved; and, whether in expressing
their opinions or in regulating their behaviour,
they cast moderation to the winds. It followed,
therefore, that Parliament, from the moment that
the fiscal apple of discord was thrown into the
arena, became a very quarrelsome and unsatis-
factory seat of judgment. Not only did this
subject fundamentally divide the two principal
parties in the State, but it sundered the Unionist
party from top to bottom, cleaving the confidence
and friendship of old associates and increasing
an hundredfold the heat of discussion. In such
an atmosphere invective, bitter and sustained, was
the common weapon employed by those who could
wield it, and Bonar was a past-master in its use.
Nor did this high flood of feeling ebb away after
the General Election of 1906; it disposed of the
question for the time being, but it left a residuum

in the shape of the worst-tempered House of Commons since 1880, a label which it bequeathed to its successors, who deserved it until the outbreak of war.

Such an atmosphere was decidedly unfavourable for teaching the doctrines of sweet reasonableness or of diplomatic speech to a man of Bonar's fibre, who conscientiously believed that he owed it to his principles and his party to call a spade a spade on every possible occasion. And it is fair to say that he was encouraged in this cruder form of political expression by the forward section of his party, whose chief objection to Mr. Balfour as their leader was that his ways were not their ways, and that they thought him too soft a general for the fiercer warfare of those days. Such a charge could not be laid to Bonar Law's account when, by an accident of fortune, he slipped into the post of leader of the party between Walter Long and Austen Chamberlain, both of whom were statesmen trained in an older school. But the change was an abrupt one from the traditional leadership of Balfour. It may have been right or wrong; it was certainly right if one believed that fever-heat and passion and the political war-spirit were the best furnaces in which to forge weapons wherewith to attack the successive Radical programmes of Mr. Asquith and his party. That

Mr. Bonar Law

A.J.B. found little to commend in these new tactics goes without saying; they were foreign to his nature and to his reading of parliamentary tradition, as, indeed, they were also to the feelings of many of his old supporters. Still, for the sake of the party, it was unfortunate that the gap between the old leader and the new should have been so wide, since it was mainly upon questions of form that they were really divided.

I have dwelt at some length upon Bonar's new parliamentary style and upon his fearless downright character for two reasons: as leader of the Opposition these were his chief claims to the confidence of his supporters at Westminster and in the country who had not, as yet, many *data* upon which to form a reasoned opinion upon his political judgment or his constructive ability. Indeed, the more cautious of them were inclined to fear lest his honest impulses were not always completely under his control and led him and his party (as in the cases of his Ulster crusade and of certain unconsidered replies to Mr. Asquith's rhetorical questions) down paths which Arthur Balfour would have declined to tread. The other reason is that his invective had in it some unfortunate ingredient, or needed some antiseptic quality, which left a sting behind in the heart and memory of those against whom it was aimed. His arrows were very sharp, but they lacked the polish of

Asquith's scholarly satire and the hearty playful-
ness with which Lloyd George hurled abuse at
the heads of his opponents. This stood him in
ill stead when the Coalition Cabinets came to be
formed under a Prime Minister in whose bosom
some of these barbs still remained and rankled
and who, in consequence, never gave Bonar Law
the confidence or the responsibilities to which he
was entitled.

Nor was it until the Lloyd George Government
was formed at the end of 1916 that Bonar really
had a chance of pulling his full weight in the
War, a weight that was considerable both on
account of the numerical strength of the party
which he led and by reason of his knowledge and
application of business methods in a Government
with a large admixture of business men. And
here a new and unexpected trait was discovered
in this hitherto assertive and self-confident character;
the old Bonar entirely disappeared and made way
for quite a different person of the same name, who
served with the utmost fidelity and success under
the very man who had been, but a few years before,
his most inflexible political enemy. These were
the days when Lloyd George's flair was seldom
at fault; his intuitions in things great and small
were positively uncanny. He knew his Bonar,
and made him Leader of the House without a
moment's hesitation, realising the out and out

loyalty of the colleague who had "taken the
shilling" in the new Ministry. And he never
had cause to regret his choice; he must often have
said to others what he said to me many times
in Paris, during his frequent absences abroad on
Conferences between 1917 and 1919: namely that he
felt he could never have carried on if he had not
had the fullest confidence in Bonar's power to
manage the House of Commons while he was
away. But few now remember how great was
the part, how heavy were the responsibilities,
which Bonar (suffering under great bereavement)
bore during those tremendous years. He trailed
the clouds, but the glory was assigned to Lloyd
George.

On a few occasions during the Peace Conference
this tired man, already beginning to show unmis-
takable signs of over-strain, flew over to Paris
to consult his chief on parliamentary affairs or to
be consulted by experts on questions connected
with the business of the War. These journeys
by air fatigued him very much and inclined to
make him irritable. They put him out of stride
with the regularity of his work at Westminster;
and he felt that, in a sense, they wasted precious
hours at a crisis when every moment was valuable
either for work or rest. "I hate these trips,"
he once complained mournfully to me. "I can't

read anything, nor see anything, nor write nor
smoke; and the noise is so deafening that I feel
too numb to think." I always felt that he took
a gloomy view of the Peace Conference, and did
not think that much good could come of it; partly
because of the enormous number of its plenipo-
tentiaries, and partly because he was convinced
that its machinery was too cumbrous and decen-
tralised to command success. Wherefore he
showed little sign of cheerfulness when he arrived
from the skies among us in the rue Nitot, or when
Lloyd George seduced him to play a game of
golf at St. Cloud, or when A.J.B. persuaded him
to make a fourth at tennis in the Bois during
those rare but necessary periods of leisure which
were occasionally vouchsafed to our representa-
tives. I doubt whether he ever got much pleasure
or relaxation from physical exercise, although he
tacitly admitted that probably it was good for
him; certainly he got none from books or music
or works of art, whose charms had no power to
soothe him; a change of mental work was (as
also in the case of Mr. Chamberlain) the panacea
for ills like his. That, no doubt, is why his harassed
look entirely vanished when he could slip away
in the evenings to the Café de la Régence, near
the Palais-Royal and play chess with some well-
known expert from a foreign land.

I have said enough to indicate that these years

of war, with their recurring private sorrows and unending grave anxieties, aged and tormented Bonar beyond the lot of most men. It might have been better for him, in the sense of prolonging his life, if he had declined the office of First Minister of the Crown after the break-up of the Coalition for which he bore a certain responsibility. But it was humanly impossible to expect a man so constituted and with Bonar's professional ambition—for politics had now become his profession—to refuse the crown thus offered. Remember, he was the man who in 1900 was so sure of himself that he could afford to say to his intimates that he would give politics " a try "; but that, if he was not in the Government within three years, he would return to his business in Glasgow. He was the man who, as a parliamentary stripling, fought a succession of giants across the floor of the House of Commons with disconcerting effect upon their reputations and self-esteem. It was he who, when he had to put his courage to the test " to win or lose it all ", accepted the leadership of the Unionist party and thus passed over the heads of elder statesmen who had grown grey in the service of the country. He had borne his part in displacing Mr. Asquith in 1916 and Mr. Lloyd George in 1921 ; he had worthily represented the Conservative party in peace and war for ten long years, not without the belief, I feel sure, that,

in the fullness of time he would become Prime
Minister of his country. Thus situated, he had
no choice but to follow where ambition led him
and to accept the laurels that he had so richly
earned. . . . Anxiously his friends watched him
at his home in Downing Street, his life slowly
ebbing away under the double strain of unremitting
work and unconquerable disease, until the end
came. It is improbable that History will record
Bonar's Government as a memorable one; but
there will be a niche, I am assured, for the remarkable
man who formed it. He was a man who sought
power, loved power, and learned to use it both
fearlessly and well.

THE DUKE OF DEVONSHIRE
1833–1908

AFTER fifty years of public service to his country, the eighth Duke of Devonshire—better known as Lord Hartington to his own generation and as " Cav " to his intimates—was gathered to his fathers in March, 1908. I have in my life-time seen many great men come and go; but I can remember no other statesman whose passing was so universally mourned or who left so wide a gap in the front rank of public life. The reason is not far to seek : his qualities were so typically English—rugged, downright and honest—so like the qualities for which we should all like to be remembered and regretted after we are gone. These were the virtues which " brought him through the other horses " from the very start of his career : which made him the trusted lieutenant, first of Mr. Gladstone, then of Lord Salisbury, and finally of Mr. Balfour. Which of us would not like to have even one of the following tributes paid to us by our colleagues after our day is done ? —the tribute of " the straightforward sincerity of his public life " ; of " inflexible integrity and simplicity of character " ; of " tranquil indifference to praise or blame "; of " righteous courage and integrity." It is not that scores of other men in public life before and since the Duke have not been honest, simple and sincere : but that the whole of his immense national influence was founded upon these qualities, and upon these alone.

From the first to last Lord Hartington had very few of those external decorations of character which give a man a start, perhaps an unfair start, in life's handicap. In appearance he was rather ungainly and loosely-built, carelessly turned out on every occasion, indistinct in speech, shy and casual in demeanour. He had, moreover, what Lord Esher has described as " a Whig hardihood in braving public opinion, and a defiance of the conventions of high society." Intellectually his was a good brain but, perhaps, a lazy and untidy one. He never had any public school training, but worked with private tutors until he went up to Cambridge : and, as he subsequently told the undergraduates when he was Chancellor, he regretted the idle time that he had spent there. He added : " All through my life I have had to work with men who thought three times as quickly as I did ; I have found this a great disadvantage."

But this disadvantage was more than counter-acted by the inherent thoroughness of the man's character; which led him, whether as a territorial magnate owning great possessions and responsibil-

THE DUKE OF DEVONSHIRE
off Cannes

ities, or as a foremost statesman, to examine every
problem from all possible angles until he was
conversant with every argument both for and against
it. What has been called " the slow grinding of
the Cavendish mind " has been of invaluable service
to the country at many crises in its history, notably
at the birth of Home Rule in 1885 and of Tariff
Reform in 1903. " The Duke " was the terror
of statesmen in a hurry. He was never in a hurry ;
generally he was late ; but when he had reached
the goal of decision he was as immovable as a
rock.

" Listen to the silent," said a recent Dean of
St. Paul's in another connection. That was the
advice taken by the people of our country with
regard to the Duke of Devonshire. In an age of
rhetoric and prolixity he was essentially a silent
man, who followed Mr. Disraeli's counsel to
potential leaders of political parties : " They should,
in their degree, be seen but not heard." Of natural
eloquence and oratorical graces he was entirely
bereft ; yet Lord Rosebery could say of him that
" we could have spared a dozen more facile rhetor-
icians for one speaker such as the Duke of Devonshire." Countless are the stories which point to
his unpreparedness or disinclination to make
speeches, which he constantly prefaced with an
indiscreet yawn : the best known of these, perhaps,
is his dream that he was addressing the House

of Lords and, when he woke up, he found that
he actually was in the middle of a speech to that
august assembly.   On another occasion, when
asked by one of the Peers why the Cabinet had
chosen to administer the Education of the country
through a Board, he answered that " he could
not for the life of him remember what the reasons
were, but he could assure their Lordships that
they were sufficient."   And so again, a few years
afterwards, when compelled to speak in the House
of Lords on the Fiscal question, he was proceeding
to enumerate Mr. Balfour's four principal points.
Three of them he could remember, but he had
forgotten the fourth.   Undismayed, he went on
to summarize three of Mr. Chamberlain's vital
arguments : but once more his memory failed him
and he could not recollect one of them.   So
with a stolid cough, he diverted his speech into
another channel.   This incident, which made no
difference whatever to the attention given to his
speech nor to the weight of influence attaching
to it, recalls a passage in the life of Lord Althorp,
with whom the Duke had much in common, when
he was Chancellor of the Exchequer.   There was
an occasion upon which it was necessary for him
to reply to a critic of his Budget, and he had taken
immense pains to tabulate a sheet of figures wherewith to refute his opponent.   But, when the time
came, he could not find the figures anywhere ;

he turned his pockets inside out—but in vain.
So he said, with a shrug of his shoulders : " This
morning I went thoroughly into this matter and
found that the right hon. gentleman is misinformed.
I have, apparently, not brought with me the paper
on which I noted down the argument, but I assure
the Committee that it was so." Loud cheers followed
this simple and honest explanation, and the word
of Lord Althorp was taken as equivalent to
mathematical demonstration of a triumphant argument.

There was a downright-ness about even these
casual lapses that endeared the Duke to the public,
who were very conscious of the same frailties in
their own intellectual make-up ; but they knew
full well that such superficial defects did not
subtract one grain of real matter from the substance or the dignity of his speeches.   The present
generation can hardly be expected to appreciate,
certainly not to remember, the incessant turmoil
in which this man's career was passed—a man
who was willing, though he had no desire, to
enter public life, for, as he once said, he was himself the most indolent man of his acquaintance.
Yet it is not too much to say that he was the founder
of the Liberal Unionist party, after he had seceded
from Mr. Gladstone over the question of Home
Rule, which he attacked with a passion that, until
then, nobody had dreamed him capable of sus-

taining. The pang of leaving his old chief and
many of his old party was a poignant one to him,
but it was the only honest course once he had
realised that "by the phrase 'Self-Government'
Mr. Gladstone and I do not mean the same thing."
Again, twenty years later, he went through the
Tariff Reform crisis in 1903, and was once more
at the head of a secession party (this time in the
Unionist ranks) because he could not understand
and therefore would not support Mr. Balfour's
attitude. "I am completely puzzled and dis-
tracted by all the arguments *pro* and *con* Free Trade
and Protection; but, whichever of them is right,
I cannot think that something which is neither,
but a little of both, can be right." This separation
was, I think, even sadder for him than that which
parted him from Mr. Gladstone; for he had much
more in common with A.J.B., and had gone through
stormier times with him, than he had ever shared
with the G.O.M.; and for a generation they had
trusted one another like brothers. It also broke
up the Liberal Unionist party of which he was so
proud, and for no definite reason of which he
could assure himself. Sadly he wrote to a friend:
"The politics of our family are rather mixed.
Victor (the present Duke) is a Balfourian; Dick
(Lord Richard Cavendish) is an out-and-out
Free Trader; and God knows what I am." Definite-
ness was his one object in life, no matter in what

sphere he sought it. Ambiguity or extravagance
in speech jarred terribly upon him. When somebody, at a civic function, unctuously declared that
" this was the proudest moment of his life," the
Duke was heard to mutter : " The proudest moment
of *my* life was when my pig won the first prize
at Skipton Fair." And when another admirer
wrote to remind him that he had sent a book to
the Duke's " gracious consort," he turned to his
secretary, and asked what on earth the man meant.
On being told that he meant the Duchess, he
growled surlily, " Then why the devil couldn't
he say so ? "

No other mentality would have suited the man
whom I was accustomed to see so frequently
lounging, with a leisurely disregard of time, into
the House of Lords to make an important speech,
a hand in one trouser pocket, and swinging his
hat with the other—with all the serene appearance
of believing that he was arriving five minutes too
early instead of half-an-hour late. His dress was
always the same—a tail-coat with broad lapels
and deep side pockets, a turn-down collar, a pair
of saggy baggy trousers and enormous boots.
At Newmarket and in the country elsewhere the
material might be of tweed but the cut was iden-
tical ; and he was conspicuous by wearing a curious
round-shaped bowler hat of a fashion which he
may have invented but which nobody copied.

Yet, with all this undesignedly artistic ruggedness, the Duke wore all these garments with a distinction of which even they could not deprive him.

He was a Whig and something of a democrat to boot ; one of the first to throw open his country house for the inspection of tourists on fixed days in the week—" I don't see how I can keep them out," he said. And, when asked to object to open-air meetings in Hyde Park, he made the sage reply : " If well-dressed people can go and meet there on week-days, I don't see why the others should not meet there on Sundays." And when the Duke " didn't see why not," he invariably supported an innovation for the good of the people, and his example was pretty generally followed by others. In this connection I remember that once he surprised Mr. Balfour considerably by his comment, when he heard that His Majesty King Edward VII had told Mr. Ritchie that " he did not approve of taxing the food of the poor and did not care who knew it." This observation of course delighted the Duke, who immediately said to A.J.B., " We must really get this man on the stump."

Such was the man to whom all kinds of people brought their troubles, from Prime Ministers downwards. He would examine them with infinite care and his advice, when he understood the case, but not before, was willingly given and generally

accepted. Indeed, such was his character for
integrity joined to the common-sense of a man
of the world, that he used jocosely to complain
that "whenever a man is caught cheating at cards,
the case is referred to me." And this was natural,
in a way, because the Duke never went very far
afield and was therefore always fairly close at hand
for consultation. Of Newmarket he was a regular
patron, and missed as few meetings as possible;
he delighted in his salmon fishing at Lismore in
Ireland, and Bolton Abbey invariably saw him
during the grouse-shooting season. These were
his principal out-of-door pleasures in his later years,
though in his younger days he had been a hard
rider to hounds. This reference to grouse-shooting
reminds me of an amusing incident of which I
was a witness long ago at Barrow-in-Furness. It
was on the occasion of the visit of the famous
Chinese Envoy Li Hung Chang to the industrial
works in that neighbourhood. The Duke, who
was living at Holker Hall, close by, was with
difficulty persuaded to go and meet Li Hung Chang
at the Station Hotel, at the unearthly hour of
eight o'clock in the morning. Both the principals
at this conclave were rather sleepy, and conversation was not exactly easy. At last, after a long
pause, Li asked the Duke (through his interpreter)
what he was doing during the parliamentary recess.
"I am shooting grouse," replied His Grace. . . .

(Pause.) . . . Ask His Excellency if he has ever shot grouse ? "

" No," was the answer. " Tell the Duke that I only shoot rebels " ; and that was the end of that conversation.

Incidentally, he was a fine pigeon shot in his youth. A very good friend of his reports that once he laid him 100–4 that he would beat him in a competition at Monte Carlo and then doubled the bet. " I thought I had caught a 'flat'; but it was a tartar—for Hartington won the match."

I do not think that the Duke worried much about foreign affairs after he had ceased to be a member of Mr. Gladstone's Cabinet; up to that time they had been the cause of constant anxiety to him, owing to the way in which they were conducted under the guidance of the G.O.M. But he travelled mildly, as far as German spas* or to Paris and the Riviera, and during the last twenty years of his life he paid a couple of visits to Egypt, more in search of health than of information. It was on the latter of these trips that he went as far as Luxor, and was there invited to drive out to Karnak to see the excavation and cleaning of the Sacred Lake, in which already many ancient treasures had been found, and where it was hoped to find more. To ensure that there should be no

---

* " The waters are all humbug," he wrote to a colleague who was at Marienbad ; "but I hope you are learning to play bridge."

disappointment, and that their Graces should experience a thrill of satisfaction, recourse was had
to the simple device of burying a gold vessel in
the sub-soil, from which it would subsequently
be recovered as a new and precious find. On
the appointed day, all was in order : an army of
naked workers were busy in the lake, and the
Duke and Duchess took the seats of honour under
the shady tent that had been prepared for them.
All went well, in spite of the great heat, and the
illustrious visitors showed keen interest in the
proceedings. An hour passed, when suddenly a
shout went up, and a native raised a beautiful
chalice high above his head ; he had recovered
it from the foundations of the lake. All eyes
turned instinctively to the Seats of the Mighty
. . . but both their Graces were fast asleep.

How true, alas, that " the best laid schemes of
mice and men gang aft agley." I do not think that
the Duke and Duchess ever heard this story, but
I was told it at Karnak two or three years ago.
A few weeks later he died in Cannes.

LORD LANSDOWNE

1845–1927

EVERY young nobleman having great possessions who is anxious to enter the public service of his country should be advised to study the career of Lord Lansdowne. It is impossible to accept this advice and not to share the admiration and affection in which he was held in Europe, Asia and America, not only whilst occupying posts of the highest responsibility in those three continents but after he had left them; it should be almost impossible not to wish to follow in his footsteps right down to the end of the life-journey of the last of the great Whig statesmen.

A Whig Lord Lansdowne was born, and a Whig by temperament he remained, whether he was serving under Mr. Gladstone in 1868, in Lord Salisbury's Government in 1895, or with Mr. Asquith in the Coalition Ministry of 1916. Mr. Balfour is credited with the humorous observation, which need not be taken too literally, that he "never knew the use of Whigs until he came to sit in Cabinet with Lansdowne." Certainly the use of Lord Lansdowne was patent from the

outset of his public career; whether as an Under-
Secretary in his early days when, under Mr. Cardwell,
he served in the War Office, or in Canada and
India as Viceroy, or, on his return home, as Secretary
of State for War and afterwards for Foreign Affairs.
Serenity, sagacity and style were three invaluable
qualities that he brought to the performance of
his duties wherever they lay, together with an
unfaltering frankness and loyalty which earned him
the complete confidence of successive Sovereigns
and colleagues. It is no wonder that, thus equipped
from his Oxford days with these essential attributes
of high character, Dr. Jowett of Balliol should
have held a great opinion of his ability and promise,
even though he only secured a " second " in his
Final Schools. This the " Master " assigned to
his pupil's want of interest in political and general
subjects and to the unfortunate fact that, during
his residence at Oxford, he had succeeded to the
inheritance of large and encumbered estates, the
responsibility for which lay heavily upon him.
But Lord Lansdowne himself made no secret of
the fact that, in those days of glorious youth,
there was not time in the twenty-four hours to
work for a " first " and also to get in all the sport
and exercise and opportunities for spirited good-
fellowship which are always knocking at the door
of a healthy undergraduate. Such pleasures,
however, were short-lived in his case, for a year

after leaving the University he entered that public life which he adorned for the next sixty years.

Perhaps I should excuse the foregoing attempt to sketch in the early years of Lord Lansdowne before I knew him by saying that in my opinion the portrait, however slight and incomplete, of a great man should bear the faintest touch of colour to indicate the glow of youth that once was his ; especially in the case of Lord Lansdowne, whose private character—so full of fun and of *joie de vivre*—was as little known to the " man in the street " as the real character of the late Lord Curzon. To the public Lord Lansdowne was unseen and almost unknown—he took infinite pains that as little as possible should be heard or seen of him by those whom he did not concern ; what they did know was that a very " safe " man with a big position in the country had been sent by Mr. Gladstone as Viceroy to Canada, where he had done admirably well, and then by Lord Salisbury to India, where he had acquitted himself even better. He had embarked on no military excursions nor caused any political alarms in either country ; so the ordinary elector, with that implicit trust which he reposed in Lord Salisbury, was prepared to believe that when Lord Lansdowne was appointed Secretary of State for War it was a good appointment, and he accepted him more by faith than by sight.

But, even when one saw him threading his way alertly to his seat on the Government Front Bench in the House of Lords, one learned little about the real man from his outward appearance. He was a small spare man, dark and dapper, with classic features, a carefully trimmed moustache and a pair of eyes that twinkled through the mask of rather a severe countenance. A figure of faultless correctitude, he stood at the box, dressed in a black or a grey frock-coat, to make a statement or a reply in that perfect parliamentary form which combines verbal polish with a frigidity of demeanour that deprecates subsequent debate. It is possible that, elsewhere than in the Second Chamber, Lord Lansdowne might have been mistaken for a foreigner, so spruce and suave was he ; but, when he began to speak, his *boutonné* manner, his staccato delivery devoid of all gesture, and his brevity made men doubt whether, indeed, he had both French and Irish blood coursing through his veins. It has been suggested that, if he could have passed a few years of apprenticeship in the House of Commons, Lord Lansdowne might have acquired some of those popular graces which can propagate great causes from the platform and carry multitudes off their feet. I have my doubts about this, for I cannot believe that either the hustings or the House of Commons could have converted Lord Lansdowne, any more than it could have turned the late Duke of Devonshire, from being a reflective and sedate individual by nature into an imaginative and enthusiastic advocate of party programmes. Indeed, I should be inclined to say that the few real Whigs that I have been privileged to know were all of them singularly devoid of this particular talent for popular appeal : men like Lord Granville, Lord Spencer and Lord Ripon, no doubt the wisest of counsellors in Cabinet, were not attractive public speakers. It almost seemed to require some radical irritant in the system, from which Whigs were generally immune but which affected Conservatives and Liberals in varying degrees, to provide the oratorical nourishment that democratic audiences were so eager to absorb.

I have asked the reader to note in passing that Lord Lansdowne's two Pro-Consular periods (in Canada and India) were calm, successful and wise years of administration, thanks to the tactful hands and the uncommon-sensible head which directed public affairs in those two great Dependencies during his terms of exile. But when they were over, and when he came home to preside over the War Office, it seemed as though the rulings of Providence were permanently given against him, and that he was to know no more peace until the end of his public life. First of all there was Army Re-organisation to claim his attention and to

THE MARQUESS OF LANSDOWNE
at Derreen

bring him into conflict with the Cabinet on questions of finance, to so grave an extent that he offered to resign. Then followed a long period of unrest : of differences with Queen Victoria on the subject of the Commander-in-Chief ; the Nile Campaign, which ended victoriously at Omdurman, and the outbreak of the Boer War which began so disastrously for the British Army, whose state of unpreparedness for a foreign campaign was most unjustly laid at Lord Lansdowne's door. Once again, in 1900, he offered to " stand aside "; but Lord Salisbury would not hear of the suggestion since, as I happen to know, he had long made up his mind that Lord Lansdowne was the right man to succeed him at the Foreign Office. This translation came as a great surprise to him, but it was a welcome change for a man of his tastes and temperament ; for one who, in spite of all his serenity, could not but feel deeply, though he would not repel, the gross injustice of the rabid attacks made on him during the course of the South African campaign, not only by opponents but by others in his own camp who ought to have known better.

But Lord Lansdowne was under no illusion as to the character of the legacy to which he had succeeded by the will of his great predecessor at the Foreign Office, perhaps the most powerful Minister of the day in Europe. He knew the atmosphere of almost universal hostility which surrounded Great Britain, partly on account of Lord Salisbury's policy of proud isolation, and partly as the result of the Boer War which very nearly united the Triple and the Dual Alliances against us. He knew, too, the inherent difficulty of carrying out a strong foreign policy at a time when the ultimate instruments of that policy— the Army and the Navy—were fully occupied thousands of miles away. And this knowledge, which was not of yesterday or the day before, brought him to lead England gently and almost imperceptibly to consider and then to embrace a change in foreign policy from one of " splendid isolation " to one of advantageous foreign alliances. It was not many months after his accession to the Foreign Office that he opened negotiations to promote an Anglo-German alliance, a proposal which came to naught owing to the impulsive and jealous incapacity of the German Foreign Minister, Prince von Bülow. An effort to improve our estranged friendship with Russia was no more successful, and the moment had not yet come to make similar advances to Italy. Thereupon Lord Lansdowne's ingenious mind switched off with lightning rapidity from West to East and, after delicate and difficult negotiations, an Anglo-Japanese Agreement was signed in February, 1902. Here the British Peace-Maker *par excellence* reaped

the first harvest of his political foresight, to the
apparent delight of the German Emperor, who
saw in it a cause of chagrin to Russia and to France,
for such it was. But Lord Lansdowne, still pursuing
his policy of conciliation (after having peacefully
solved the question of Russian encroachments in
Persia, the somewhat delicate difference with King
Edward as to whether the Shah of Persia was or
was not to be given the Order of the Garter, and
other important controversies, involving the United
States, upon such matters as the Venezuelan
question and the Alaskan boundaries), was not
to be deterred from endeavouring to make friends
with the Dual Alliance, if industry and perseverance
and the arts of diplomacy could bring about a
consummation so desirable for the peace of the
world. As we know, with regard to France, this was
brilliantly achieved by him, after long months of
negotiation, and an Anglo-French agreement became
a *fait accompli* in April, 1904. His, and not entirely
King Edward's, was the policy of the Entente
Cordiale ; and to him and to M. Paul Cambon the
main credit must be gladly given. Something of
a similar kind might have been arranged with
Russia, if that country had possessed statesmen of
the same calibre and integrity as the French, and
if the Czar had been proof against the Anglophobe
machinations of the German Emperor, whose
whole influence was concentrated upon making

the Emperor of Russia believe that England was assisting the Japanese to win the war against him. Nevertheless the good seed was scattered, and in 1907 Sir Edward Grey reaped an Anglo-Russian Agreement where Lord Lansdowne had sown.

In 1905, at the comparatively early age of sixty, Lord Lansdowne completed his term as Foreign Secretary, having already held three of the highest offices under the Crown. Those were five important years (1900–1905) in our country's history, to which Lord Lansdowne had helped to contribute a new chapter at the opening of the new century. Nor should it be forgotten that, whilst he was deeply occupied in framing a new foreign policy and in carrying it out, he was also immersed in the stormy flood of Fiscal Reform polemics and in the Irish Devolution question which caused George Wyndham to resign from the Cabinet. One can well believe that, after the General Election of 1905, he was far from unwilling to abandon " the sweets of office " (?) and to exchange them for the congenial pursuits of breeding pigs at Bowood and catching salmon in Ireland. But his freedom to enjoy the life of a private citizen was of short duration for, on the death of the Duke of Devonshire in 1908, the duty of leading the Opposition devolved upon him in the House of Lords, and of piloting the Unionist Peers through the storms that gathered round the Lloyd George Budget of 1909 and which finally broke when the Parliament Bill was carried through Parliament. And so, quietly and without fuss, but always at the head of his big battalions, this serene and sagacious statesman passed from one crisis to another until, in 1914, all domestic crises were swallowed up in the world-cataclysm of the Great War: all old landmarks seemed to disappear; only the foreign policy of Lord Lansdowne remained unshaken and unchanged.

From this period onwards, Lord Lansdowne seemed to relax his interest in public affairs. He was over seventy years old, his health had begun to fail, and he had been numbed by the shattering blow of the death of his second son, Lord Charles Mercer-Nairne, who was killed in action. Nevertheless, largely through Mr. Balfour's desire that he should do so, he joined the Second Coalition Cabinet in 1916 and circulated to his colleagues a Memorandum on the subject of possible proposals which might lead to an early peace; a State Paper which, in the following year (1917), appeared— quite unexpectedly—as the famous Peace Letter in the *Daily Telegraph*. The merits of this striking document have been so much canvassed and criticised that I need not dwell upon them here; history must decide in its own good time whether this pronouncement was helpful or harmful, wise or otherwise, expedient or inopportune. But this certainly may be said : that every line of it shows the passion for peace which was always the ruling feature of Lord Lansdowne's character, whether in public or private affairs, and which left its indelible mark upon his administrations both at home and abroad.

Soon after this, in 1919, he was overtaken by serious illness which he bore with uncomplaining fortitude, but which laid him aside for a long time and precluded him from taking part in public affairs. It changed his appearance very much, but not his innate courtesy and consideration for all sorts and conditions of men, nor his love of country life both in England and Ireland, nor his immense influence over the House of Lords, where he made his last speech in 1925, though he attended regularly until within a fortnight of his death in 1927.

The end came quietly, as one can well believe that he would have wished; and the last of the Whig statesmen passed to his rest, full of years and of honour, mourned as he was admired by all who knew him in work or play. He was a " very perfect Knight," a scholar in the best sense of the word, who had declined the high distinction of being Chancellor of Oxford University and suggested the name of Lord Curzon who accepted it. He was a keen patron of the Arts and a devoted lover of nature in the wild. Of friends he made a multitude, gathered from all parts of the world, but of intimates he had few. So far as I know he never had a nickname, and the only people (outside the older members of his own family) by whom I heard him addressed as " Clan " were the late Duke of Devonshire, Arthur Balfour —his fag at Eton—and Lord Rosebery, his close particular friend at Oxford. For his family he kept the very best that was in him ; and Lady Lansdowne, his brilliant and inseparable partner throughout a long honeymoon of married life, lived in the very shrine of his heart. None of these, nor the ghillies nor the gardeners, nor the Indian bearers, nor the Canadian *voyageurs* who worshipped him, need to be told the enduring worth of this stainless life ; and I think that posterity, whose judgment is now upon the men of those times, having read Lord Lansdowne's record of 'things done', will be hard put to it to find a finer champion of the British watchword " *Noblesse oblige.*"

MR. JOSEPH CHAMBERLAIN
1836–1914

To those who are elected as members of the House of Commons for the first time, that august institution is not only the best club in London but it is something of a " raree show " as well. I hope that this statement may still be true; it was certainly accurate in the year 1895 when I first passed through the swing-doors and faced the Speaker's chair. We were quite alive to the fact that now we were clothed with dignity as children of the Mother of Parliaments; but at the same time we were consumed with curiosity to see and hear and know, with a friendly smoking-room knowledge, our elder brothers who had already made history. True, we had just missed the great honour of being able to say that we had sat in the House with Mr. Gladstone, or had listened to Lord Randolph's invective or to Speaker Peel's terrific admonitions; for these gentlemen had belonged to the previous Parliament and had passed with it. But we were agog to become " honourable friends " to some and " honourable gentlemen " to others whose names were already household words throughout the country. There was Keir

Hardie, for instance, whose arrival in a char-à-
banc to take his seat, wearing a cloth cap and
accompanied by a brass-band to the doors of
Westminster, was still a stirring memory. And
John Burns, whom we connected with the reddest
of red revolutionaries and riots in Trafalgar Square,
but who mellowed later into the most conservative of democratic Ministers, the soldiers' friend,
and an ardent collector of old books about London.
Then there was Sir William Harcourt, burly and
boisterous, to whose strained relations with Lord
Rosebery we were largely indebted for the upset
of the Liberals and our own election to Parliament ;
there was Asquith, on the threshold of a great
career ; Colonel Saunderson, the hero of the great
Home Rule fight on the floor of the House, and
many another popular figure. Chief of all perhaps,
after our leader Arthur Balfour, we wanted to
watch at close quarters the parliamentary talents
displayed by Mr. Joseph Chamberlain, now in
the Unionist Government but, not so long ago,
our (Tory) embodiment of everything that was
politically satanic. We had read of him (in our
own organs of the Press) as the erstwhile " Repub-
lican " Mayor of Birmingham, the truculent assailant
of the aristocracy in general and of the House of
Lords in particular. A few years passed, and we
applauded his split from the Radicals over Home
Rule and his nightly duels with his old leader

Mr. Gladstone. Now we were to admire him, as a leader of the Unionist party; a full-blooded Imperialist and perhaps the best administrator who ever presided over the Colonial Office. What manner of man was this, who could change his party, and apparently his principles, without losing dignity or character or old personal friends?

I sat close behind Mr. Chamberlain, on the seats in rear of the Treasury bench, for six years, and had every opportunity of watching his prowess as, what Sir William Harcourt used to call, "a House o' Commons man." Look back to the old caricatures of him by F. C. Gould and you will never forget his outward appearance. A sallow, keen, clean-shaved face—rather like Mr. Pitt with an eye-glass, though Lord Rosebery always vehemently denied the resemblance; sloping shoulders supporting a thick neck that seemed to be bent a little forward and to push his face into a sort of peering position : a neat figure of medium height, well-groomed; a general impression of youth, alertness and spring. And yet he did not deserve to give this impression; for he once told me that all the physical exercise he ever took consisted in walking up to and down from his bedroom in Princes' Gardens ; "You smoke far too much," said an American doctor to him. "Yes, I know," was the answer; "but then you see I never take any exercise." But this did not prevent him from

eating, drinking and smoking as much as he wanted
to, without any ill-effects upon his health or his
power of work. I can see him now, as the summer
morning was breaking upon an all-night sitting,
eating devilled bones, drinking a genial mixture
of stout and champagne, and discussing politics
over a black cigar with all the verve and cheer-
ful wide-awakeness of a much younger man.
That was in the days when all-night sittings
succeeded one another almost as regularly as the
dawns.

One used to be told of the surprise with which
the House of Commons heard Mr. Chamberlain's
maiden speech. Both sides had anticipated an
outpouring of fire and brimstone and sudden death
—such was the legendary reputation of the terrible
Mayor of radical Birmingham. Instead of which
. . . a quiet, well-ordered oration, perfect in
parliamentary form, and admirably delivered in a
voice that had been trained to public speaking and
could use every inflexion of it with precise effect.
He needed no artifice to arrest attention and keep
it while he was on his legs ; imagery was as foreign
to his style as were quotations from the classics
or the exuberant action of many orators of that
day. In all respects he was one of the quietest
speakers to whom I have ever listened—and his
deadliest thrusts were delivered almost in a whisper.

H

Two of his gestures became very familiar to us all : when he was approaching a prepared reply to a considered argument, which he carefully repeated, he used to give a little shrug to his shoulders and a hitch to his coat, as though to free his muscles for the bout that was to follow. And when he was interrupted, he fixed his monocle very deliberately in his eye, leaned forward intently with finger outstretched in the direction of his opponent, purred out his pungent repartee, then sprang back to the upright, polished his glass with his handkerchief, and waited impassive until the tumult ceased.

It is a truism to say that very few Ministers shine with equal brilliance in statement and in debate ; different qualities are required for each of these exercises. But Mr. Chamberlain managed to combine them to an exceptional degree, and to invest long and complicated pronouncements of policy with peculiar interest, due partly to his complete mastery of structure, and partly to that lucidity of language which is the accompaniment of cold clear thinking. Of his supreme debating powers I have already said something and will only add that, even at the end of an exhausting day, they never seemed to fail him ; his rapier was still sharp, his aim as deadly at five in the morning as it had been when the engagement began on the previous afternoon.

The art of public speaking was a subject which interested Mr. Chamberlain and to which he had given a good deal of attention. It was said, I know not with how much truth, that in his youth he had studied elocution for the purposes of private theatricals; that might account for his wonderful enunciation and for an excellence of voice production that it was a pleasure to hear. I remember his summing-up of the best kind of speech for House of Commons purposes : he said it should be short, full of substance, and spoken as easily as conversation in a smoking-room. That was thirty years ago, and I do not think that better advice could be given to-day. Mr. Chamberlain often came to the weekly dinners of our "Hughligan" club in the House. On one occasion, I remember, we were rather nervous about receiving him because, only a couple of hours previously, we had clashed swords with the Prime Minister (Mr. Balfour) over some incident at the close of the Boer War, and the sound of battle had not quite died away by dinner time. However, at the appointed hour, our guest turned up, debonair and smiling, yet with a mischievous twinkle in his eye. He opened fire on us at once : "That was a fine skirmish of yours in the House this afternoon. I hope you enjoyed it. By the way, has your little gang any principles at all and, if so, what are they?" To which Lord Percy—replying more particularly for Hugh Cecil, Winston and himself—said, " Purity, Parsimony and the Persian Gulf." " I see," murmured our guest reflectively : " I thought they might be " Pushfulness, Person alities and the Press."

Then he went on to say : " Why don't you young men take up some cause really worth fighting for, such as the protection of our markets against world-competition, and a closer economic union with the Colonies ? " ; and for an hour, I suppose, we listened to an impromptu outline of his scheme of Tariff Reform. Many times in after years I heard him say that the first time he ever mentioned that thorny subject inside the House of Commons was at that Hughligan dinner. How it developed into a political problem of predominant and over-shadowing interest for the Unionist party needs no explaining. I went with Mr. Chamberlain to many meetings, at Birmingham, Edinburgh and elsewhere, to hear his expositions of the gospel which he had made his own ; always the same methods were used, even before critical or hostile audiences ; close reasoning, calm delivery and an " easy smoking-room conversational " style, which riveted the attention even of his most implacable opponents and made them impatient of uproarious dissent.

It was said of Mr. Chamberlain after his death, by one of those who knew him best, Lord Morley,

Mr. Joseph Chamberlain
at Highbury

that he had a genius for friendship; and what finer tribute could be paid to the character of any man? For here was a politician who lived in an age when party feeling ran tempestuously high, who agreed violently and disagreed violently; who saw around him the wreckage of private friendships and old associations shattered on the rocks of political strife; who changed his allegiance and carried his chief supporters with him into the opposing camp but—never lost a friend! Many wiser heads than mine have tried to define the warp and the woof of friendship; or, to change the metaphor, to name the spark that inspires it and the fuel that keeps it burning. Is it community of tastes and interests that attracts two men to one another, or does opposite call to opposite across the gulf of solitude? I know not; certainly, in the case of Mr. Chamberlain, I would not hazard a guess, for I can claim no title to have had more than a long acquaintance with him. But it was near enough to admire his genius for friendship, especially old friendship, and his unswerving loyalty to those who served him and his policy whether at home or abroad. I do not think that in my day he made many new friends, in the intimate sense of the word, though he gained a devoted army of supporters ready to go through fire and water at his bidding. Perhaps, outside politics, he did not share many tastes and leisured occu-

pations with men who were not his old colleagues
and contemporaries ; the general impression being
that, when he had any spare time, he devoted it
to the more solitary pursuits of gardening and
reading in his library. Of his trusted henchmen
in the House, I have the keenest recollection of
two, who gave him loyal service and devotion
such as few leaders can have enjoyed. The first
of these was Powell-Williams ; a grey-haired, rosy-
faced, benevolent old gentleman with a bland and
child-like smile. He was a great favourite in the
House, where he was universally known by the
ludicrously inappropriate name of " Mars " (due
to his appointment as Financial Secretary to the
War Office) for he was the least war-like of all
the tribe of Birmingham. Powell-Williams was
Mr. Chamberlain's " little oil bath " ; and to him
was due in large part the smooth running and the
efficiency of the Liberal Unionist organisation.
The other ' fidus Achates ' with whom Mr. Chamberlain was on intimate and affectionate terms was
Jesse Collings (of " three acres and a cow " fame)
whose appearance was like a patriarchal pantaloon,*
and who, by his public speeches and private advice,
was *persona grata* in agricultural constituencies.
Both of these men had worked for their Chief in
the days of his municipal glory ; and he did not

*A teacher in a Sunday School class at Birmingham asked one of
his pupils " Who was David " ? The answer was immediately forth-
coming : " The son of Jesse Collings."

forget them when Unionist Ministries came to be formed thereafter.

So it was also with those who served him in the Colonial Office, whether as Governors abroad or as permanent officials at home; no men ever worked for a more loyal Chief or for a more single-minded champion of his subordinates. I had one small personal experience of Mr. Chamberlain's power of defence—which was generally attack. I had come back from some long journey abroad where I had formed a poor opinion of a certain Governor whom the Colonial Secretary had never even seen. This view, and the evidence for it, I communicated to Mr. Chamberlain who let me understand, in unequivocal language, that, if my criticisms were well founded, they would certainly have reached him long ago and the peccant official would have been removed; but that as nothing of the kind *had* reached him, I had better withdraw my observations and attend to my own business. No man, I suppose, ever used stronger language more deliberately than " Joe," whether to support a friend or to confound a foe. It was so in the days of the Tariff Reform controversy, when all of us " Free Fooders," under Hicks-Beach and the Duke of Devonshire, found ourselves in the opposite camp to the high-priest of the new gospel. He scourged us in the House, pursued us in our constituencies, denounced us from the platform

. . . but he never lost a friend. It was the deep
sincerity and conviction in Joseph Chamberlain's
character that carried him triumphant over tidal
changes of opinion and through political whirlpools
that would have drowned the reputation of a lesser
man. It did more ; for it not only lifted him over
the

"stepping-stones
"Of his dead self to higher things ",

but it bore his political friends with him ; it utterly
confounded the old view that because a man, in
changed circumstances, changed his opinion, that
man was therefore dishonest, ambitious or untrust-
worthy. Some day, and soon I hope, we shall
have the biography of Joseph Chamberlain before
us. It will be a lasting monument to a sane
Imperialist, a Greater Englander and a staunch
friend.

SIR WILLIAM HARCOURT
1827–1904

I COUNT it a great privilege to have sat in the House of Commons with Sir William Harcourt, for he was one of the last of the great Early Victorians left to serve and adorn it. He delighted in it, and it in him. When I got there, he had already been an M.P. for close on thirty years, with a variegated career behind him. He had been a lawyer who was reputed to know very little law; but he had, nevertheless, made a substantial name for himself by contributing letters (as " Historicus ") to *The Times*, on recognising the belligerent rights of the Southern States in the American Civil War, and had also added the sum of about £40,000 to his own modest fortune during the ten years that he practised at the Parliamentary Bar. He had been a politician with Liberal leanings and ambitions; but he did not care a great deal about Mr. Gladstone nor very much about modern Liberal principles, and had actually flirted with Disraeli in the shade until Mr. Gladstone made him Solicitor-General in 1873. Then, after another period of political infidelity, he made it up with Mr. Gladstone, though he fell out with others,

became his Home Secretary in the 1880 Parliament,
and did yeoman service for the Liberal party during
the next twenty-five years. Such were his political
antecedents when first I saw him—a gigantic,
broad-shouldered, loose-limbed figure, with a small
head, a large nose and a protuberant under-lip,
small eyes and gold-rimmed glasses, over which
he peered much oftener than he looked through
them. Everything was broad about Sir William,
except his head and, perhaps, his heart. His
principles were broad—broader than his politics,
which he once described as " the politics of a
younger son " ; his back was broad, his humour
was broad, and his chuckle at his own jokes was
broadest of all. He enjoyed excellent health, and
at the age of seventy we found him joining daily
in the rough and tumble of debate with the enthusiasm of a boisterous schoolboy. In controversy,
as Oscar Wilde said of somebody else, he " played
the Rugby game." And when, in 1898, he got
clear of the Rosebery entanglement, he was happier
still ; an emancipated Father O'Flynn (with a dash
of the Vicar of Bray), laying about him right and
left, fore and aft, with criticism and invective
and old-fashioned quips, and rollicking over his
performances like a shire-horse in a hayfield. With
all these popular accomplishments at his disposal,
Harcourt, or " Jumbo " as he was nicknamed,
ought to have been an ideal leader of the Liberal

SIR WILLIAM HARCOURT

[*Haines*

party in succession to Mr. Gladstone. For he was an expert in party management or " business," a master of the rules of the House of Commons and a man of long parliamentary experience. Yet somehow he failed. Partly his failure was due, I think, to his temper which was short and uncertain; his jibes had a sting in them that was not easily forgotten or forgiven; and his trouncings of a political opponent or of a recalcitrant Radical were too heavy and too long. Again; though his speeches were good and sometimes excellent, until he began to read them, he seldom gave the impression, either in the House or on the platform, that he was heart and soul in the cause that he was advocating. He could easily lash the Tories to fury with his denunciation; but the same speech did not inspire his supporters to " die in the last ditch " for him in the way that a less provocative but more convinced debater might have done. And then he had the reputation, which was not altogether unfounded, of being very jealous for his own position and advancement, very intolerant of a rival on the steps of the throne that he hoped to occupy. That made him a bad political bedfellow and accounted for a good deal of the trouble that arose in the Liberal party. But it is only fair to say that he had good cause for the divine discontent that embittered him in public. I am told that, during Mr. Gladstone's long absences from

Parliament in Disraeli's last Administration, Harcourt had good reason to hope that he might be chosen to lead the Opposition; but Lord Hartington was preferred before him. So again, in 1894, after Harcourt had been Mr. Gladstone's first lieutenant for twelve years, the Grand Old Man retired : what more natural than that he should have stepped into his leader's shoes ? But luck once more was against him ; this time it was Lord Rosebery who was sent for to kiss hands at Windsor as Prime Minister.

The House of Commons is a strange place, very critical but very just towards its members. On this occasion it felt corporately that it had been passed over without good cause, and that some influence which ought not to have operated had nevertheless been effective in denying the claims of one of its oldest, most industrious and most devoted members. This feeling, more abstract perhaps than personal, expressed itself by a great show of sympathy for Harcourt, which was not a propitious omen for Lord Rosebery's first Administration. For Harcourt, with all his parliamentary experience, was a bad loser ; and, backed by considerable numerical support from his own rank and file, he succeeded in making the Prime Minister's path a *via dolorosa* until that Parliament came to an end. From this time onward he seemed to lose some of his buoyancy ; he was defeated at Derby by a young and untried Conservative, but was immediately afterwards elected for West Monmouth, and returned to Westminster to lead a decimated and disgruntled party in the autumn of 1895. But there was little left for him to do, after he and John Morley retired in 1898 from the joint leadership of the Liberal party, except to write Erastian letters to *The Times* on Church Discipline, to gird at us during the Boer War, and to poke quite adequate fun at the Conservatives over their Tariff Reform differences. Be it said that he did all of these things with fine spirit and evident pleasure, which his opponents were able to share; for his power, even of mischief, was almost gone, although he was still a brave old swashbuckling figure who revelled in the smell of powder and the sound of Parliamentary battle. When his end came, all that might have been remembered against him was forgotten, at any rate on the Conservative side, and his personality was sorely missed. It was, in a sense, a dramatic end; for no sooner had he announced his intention (in March 1904) of resigning his seat at the next General Election than he succeeded to the family estates of Nuneham. When answering a letter of congratulation on his succession, he gaily replied that he was going to devote the rest of his life to the repeal of his own Hares and Rabbits Act and of his own famous Death Duties of 1894. All his old friends hoped that there, after a strenuous life, this scion of the Plantagenets—an aristocratic autocratic Whig, if ever there was one—would enjoy a leisured old age in his gardens and among his books. But it was not to be. Six months later " the stately column broke," and the Death Duties which he had laid upon the backs of the landed gentry in 1894 fell heavily upon the shoulders of his eldest son. Thus passed out of our sight a very remarkable figure in the political and social world of the nineteenth century ; a fine scholar, an acknowledged wit, a brilliant conversationalist and an ardent House of Commons man. Whether or not his name will go down to posterity as a statesman, who can tell ? But there are at least two tributes worth having which are his already : a tribute of gratitude from all the young men whom he loved to be with and to instruct in the faith that was in him ; and a tribute of affection, even of adoration, from his family to whom he was an idolised father and an understanding friend.

LORD MORLEY*

1838–1923

I HAVE known few men in Parliament during my lifetime who gave me the impression that they would go singing to the stake in defence of causes which they had made their own. John Morley was one of them.

If one had not learned by long experience that character is the golden key which opens the door to parliamentary triumph and political success, far transcending gifts of eloquence or dialectic or brilliance, one might wonder why Mr. Morley, from the first, reaped so many victories at Westminster. He had not sown there, but in the very different field of letters ; yet, from his maiden speech onward, he was assured of a full house and a sustained interest whenever he intervened in debate. He had not been trained to administration of any kind ; but, having accepted office and a seat in Mr. Gladstone's Cabinet as Chief Secretary for Ireland, he more than fulfilled the hopes and expectations of the Liberal party and of the Nationalists in his government of that country. He had

*Created Viscount Morley of Blackburn, 1908.

not aped the arts and artifices of platform speaking
—the high colouring or the low tones, the *sup-
pressio veri* or the *suggestio falsi* of the practised
propagandist—these were wholly alien to his
nature ; nevertheless men flocked in their hundreds
(or thousands if there was room) to listen to this
inspired democrat in his dark jacket and saffron
coloured trousers, his low collar and his reddish
bow-tie, this modern Savonarola preaching his
ascetic gospel of individual liberty and collective
effort and universal peace.

John Morley and Edward Carson (to whom, as
he is happily still with us, I will not further allude)
were two of the most austere men in politics that
it has been my good fortune to meet. But, doffed
of their respective political harness, they were both
delightfully human. Carson, with his grim features,
has a heart of gold and a devotion which, perhaps,
Arthur Balfour and Ulster knew best of all. Morley
—well, you should have seen him melting before
the influence of beautiful music, or pleading (in
private) the cause of Dreyfus with Sarah Bernhardt,
or bandying " brilliant nonsense " with Oscar
Wilde, and you would have discovered the heart
that was hidden from the world.

I delighted in his House of Commons speaking,
with its rich North country burr, his parliamentary
style, his natural way of bringing the library
temperament into his public utterances and of

[*Daily Sketch*

VISCOUNT MORLEY OF BLACKBURN

debating *sans peur et sans reproche*. None of it was studied; none of it was laboured. If he was asked why he said so-and-so, which had either neddlessly irritated his opponents or embarrassed his supporters, his answer was " I said it because I thought it "; and the enquirer was satisfied and silenced. It was of his core and fibre to be downright, sometimes perhaps unnecessarily so, especially in his books. Whatever his hand found to write or his tongue to speak, he wrote or said it with all his might. To him black was very black and white very white. There was no " perhaps " to qualify Morley's opinions. It might almost be said of him, as Dr. Johnson said of a literary rival, that he could be abstinent but not temperate. But this is not to say that he was ever silent on matters which he considered of cardinal importance to human welfare, or where he believed that his voice could influence opinion in the right direction. Far oftener than not, John Morley took the unpopular side in great events and upheld it with the conviction of a martyr. His training in the school of letters had developed his innate independence of thought and his courage; it had taught him the value of cold criticism, the dangers of enthusiasm and the snare of popular applause. And so he presented himself to his fellow-countrymen; an ascetic student of affairs, whose early life had been spent in examining and

I

writing the lives of personalities in the worlds
of politics and literature, and whose maturity was
now devoted to applying to modern conditions
the principles which had become the foundations
of his belief, with the single-hearted purpose of
bettering the state of mankind. Whether you
agreed or disagreed with his opinions did not
matter a rush to him. His intellectual inheritance
was a sword of progress and reform, and his duty
was to pass it on to succeeding generations. It
was the glowing sincerity of his purpose that
earned for him the admiration of many and the
respect of all.

Men have often wondered from what motive
this austere and simple soul, this stern, unbending
democrat, allowed himself to accept the style and
title of a Lord of Parliament ; how came it about
that " honest John " turned into Lord Morley
of Blackburn in the evening of his days ? Had
he then, for all his austerity, something of the
worldly ambition which is the common attribute
of ordinary folk ? The answer given by those
who saw most of him in his later years is that he
certainly was ambitious, in the sense of desiring
for himself all that could enhance the historic
dignity of the high offices which he adorned, and
even sensitive and impatient of any personal slight
however unintentional. His own opinion on this
subject is worth quoting :

" It is always the most difficult thing in the world to draw a line between arrogant egoism on the one hand, and on the other the identification of a man's personal elevation with the success of his public cause. The two ends probably become mixed in his mind, and, if the cause be a good one, it is the height of pharisaical folly to quarrel with him because he desires that his authority and renown shall receive some of the lustre of a far-shining triumph."

I seem to read in the foregoing a partial solution of the puzzle of his translation to the Lords. It may also account for his insistence, although in vain, that Lord Curzon should be raised to the English Peerage on his return from India as Viceroy, in order to mark the continuing dignity of an occupant of that great Office. But it remains to be said that John Morley, whatever his political opinions, was an intellectual autocrat; and that he did care intensely for the supremacy of his doctrines that they should prevail, and that their promoters should take high rank above their fellows in the esteem of the world's workers. He valued at great worth the academic honours bestowed on him by ancient seats of learning, and he welcomed the laurel wreaths offered to him in recognition of his culture. To such a temperament it was neither unseemly nor inconvenient, nor of any great moment, that he should transfer his activities from the green benches of the Commons to the red benches of the Lords, which was the only change that, in reality, occurred. For nothing of him remained to be ennobled but his name. His character for firm administration, slow in deliberation but inflexible in action after decision, continued: his speeches always produced the same impression of a wise man thinking aloud in beautiful English and making all men agree in this, if in nothing else, that: " It makes all the difference in the world whether we put Truth in the first place or in the second." Of him it was written during his life-time by one of his admirers : " He has often been on the losing side; sometimes, perhaps, on the wrong side; never on the side of wrong."

LORD CURZON*

1859–1925

SOME years ago it was the fashion among a certain class of Oxford undergraduate to make fun of Lord Curzon—one of the few great and active Chancellors who ever really served that ancient University. It was not on account of his alleged pomposities and conceits, those inventions of middle-aged journalists and young radical dons, that they laughed at him; nor to show their youthful abhorrence of his " Caesarism " when Viceroy in India—concerning the details of which they were creditably ignorant; nor yet to register their Tory suspicions of a new broom, in the disguise of a brilliant and benevolent Chancellor, whose object it was, having carried some sweeping reforms through the Council, to create a new god in his own image and call it Oxford University. It was for none of these reasons that they derided him; but because of an unfortunate and satanic rhyme, written in a mischievous moment by one of Curzon's closest friends in their undergraduate days, for the amusement of an Oxford dining-club :

* Created Baron Curzon of Kedleston, 1898.

" My name is George Nathaniel Curzon,
    I am a most superior person," etc.,

which stuck to him like a burr through life ; it
remains the inscription shadowed underneath the
mental portrait of him as conceived by the general
public long years after his death.*

But there is another and a truer picture of Curzon
drawn by his own hand. When he went up to
Oxford he was not rich, he was not strong, he
thought he was not popular and believed he had
a middle-class mind. Yet, in spite of all these
drawbacks, imaginary or real, he was *determined*,
even then, to be Viceroy of India before he died.
I have italicised the word *determined*, because
determination, rare and ruthless, was the foundation
and the force of Curzon's character.

It is too much to hope that even Lord Ronald-
shay's admirable biography of the man—still less
the minor appreciations of him by those who knew
him best—will ever completely succeed in correcting
the popular misconceptions of that difficult personality. Nor is it of great importance to Curzon's
memory whether they are corrected or whether
they persist ; for the work that he did in and for
India will remain, *aere perennius*, so long as that great
Dependency remains a jewel in the British Crown.

*(" Like the musk in the mortar of St. Sophia at Constantinople,
it is destined to last as long as the fabric."—E. T. Raymond.)

My title to write about him lies in having worked with him in the Foreign Office when he was Under-Secretary (1895–98), and in Parliament until he went to India. Subsequently I was attached for some months to his Staff when Viceroy and, on his return to this country, heart-broken and dis-owned, we continued to work as Chief and secre-tary for many years afterwards and as friends until he died.

Just as there were many Roseberys and many Balfours, so there were at least two George Curzons, a private gentleman and a public character bearing the same name. I have always contended that unless a man knew Curzon in private life he could not possibly form a true estimate of him, nor correct that caricature of his real self which he so often presented to the public. When I entered Parliament as a young man he was already some way up the ladder of fame, owing to a short but successful tenure of office as Under-Secretary for India, and to a succession of telling speeches against the Liberal Government between the years 1892–95. He was tall and pink and sleek (as the old rhyme avers), carefully dressed in the long black frock-coat which was *de rigueur* in those days, and equally careful in his deportment and language. It is no disparagement of him to say that he took himself very seriously indeed; for by so doing he compelled others to do the same, and imposed himself upon the attention of authority at a much earlier age than most young members. As Professor Rothenstein says of Mr. Bernard Shaw : " He did not wait until he was famous to behave as a great man." It was not only his manner that was weighty, deliberate and important ; that would soon have been discounted if the content of his speeches had not been up to the confident style of their delivery. But the House soon discovered that young Curzon (like the old Curzon of later years) never spoke on any subject of which he had not made himself a master, or concerning which he was not likely to know as much as or more than most of his audience. His style was of the florid, eighteenth-century type, his voice and articulation were majestically clear ; and if he appeared to lay something like pontifical stress upon everything that he said, it was only because he lacked in some degree the sense of proportion to discriminate between matters of greater or lesser importance —not only in public speaking, but in most of the affairs of daily life. His general attitude in Parliament was that of a student, an expert, a man of tremendous drive and industry. His fellow-members were there to listen and learn, and he was there to teach them ; otherwise why waste one's time there, when one might be more profitably employed in writing books or in foreign travel. So he did not frequent the smoking-room

or the tea-room much ; he was generally to be
found reading in the library or, when raised to
Office, working in one of the dark little rooms
below stairs which were the portions of under-
secretaries. He was greatly sought after in
London society, where he was regarded not only
as " the coming man," but as a meteor of brilliant
wit and audacity who could easily outshine all
of his contemporaries and many of his elders.
He had made his name as a traveller far and wide,
had written books displaying real knowledge and
political insight, and had proved himself a sportsman of no mean order in distant lands. He was
an admirable *raconteur*, easy and humorous and
racy, a ready improvisor of light rhymes and practical jokes—in a word, a man whom everybody,
whether male or female, liked to have in a house-
party or as a neighbour at dinner. The feasts
which he organised at the Bachelors' Club for
" the Souls " ; his escapades and Rabelaisian im-
promptus during the summer sessions of the
" Crabbet Club "* under the genial presidency of
Wilfrid Blunt; his tearing spirits when on holiday
at home or abroad—these things are old but
cherished memories of him among those who knew
him best. And they knew also of his persistent
ill-health, disguise it as he might : of the spinal

---

* Its character may be guessed (perhaps wrongly) by one of its
rules: " Any one becoming a Cabinet Minister or a Bishop ceases *ipso facto*
to be a member."

weakness which forced him to wear metal supports round his body; of the lung trouble which, in his most joyous years, drove him every winter to seek recovery at Davos or St. Moritz. These disabilities, borne with uncomplaining fortitude, only endeared him the more to his friends whom he never bored by discussing the weariness of his flesh; such was his determination to add his quota to the gaiety of nations. That was the Curzon who never changed; though, with advancing years and increased responsibilities and not much better health to bear either of these burdens, his conversation did become more spacious, his humour less natural, his geniality more restricted to old friends. But when he was in their company, all sign of age and dignity and responsibility vanished and we were back once more in the old House of Commons days, one of which I shall always remember. It was the occasion of an all-night sitting to discuss some exceedingly dull subject. Curzon had been hard at work all day and, when evening was come, his soul cried out for amusement. So, about midnight, he invited a number of his friends, one by one, to go down to his room for a whisky and soda and a sandwich. Now in that room was a particular chair, whose venerable seat collapsed through its frame whenever it was sat upon. His guests came down singly; each was guided to that chair with the

LORD CURZON
in Burma

inevitable result : a crash, a disconcerted victim
and a peal of laughter from his host. The guests,
of course, all remained to see the trick repeated
on their successors. The last to arrive was Haldane,
whose staid appearance and burly form promised
the maximum of amusement. He rolled genially
into the room, now crowded to overflowing, but
fortunately there was one chair unoccupied. Into
it he sank ; through he went, " bringing the
House down " with shouts of delight as he vainly
tried to extricate himself. Curzon was enchanted.
On another occasion he was no less amused when
the tables were turned against himself. We were
shooting at Hackwood and, at luncheon time, we
found ourselves in the schoolmaster's parlour
adjoining the village school. It occurred to
Curzon to send a message into the next room to
say that, after luncheon, General Baden-Powell
would address the scholars on the Boy-Scout
movement. He then informed Lord Newton (to
our great satisfaction) that he was to impersonate
the General and to make the best speech he could.
All went off splendidly, and a thundering cheer
greeted his closing remarks which we were not
privileged to hear. On Lord Newton's return we
asked what he had said to get such rapturous
applause. " I only said that I wanted a whole
holiday for the boys to mark this occasion, and
that Curzon hoped they would all spend it in

his park and he would give them tea afterwards."
Thus was the biter bit.

At bottom Curzon was a reserved man, with
an " inferiority complex " quite at variance with
the pompous and arrogant conception of him
which is still so prevalent. He had a lack of
confidence in his fellow-creatures which was
inexplicable, except for the double reason that
(as I have already said) he imagined that he was
not popular ; and then the , having had to do
everything for himself as a young man (even to
mending his own trousers and sewing the buttons
on to his own boots) he was innately shy of asking
anyone to do things for him. It was not a far step
from this drawback to the belief, which he resolutely
held and expressed : that " if you want a thing well
done, you must do it yourself." Who can blame
onlookers if they mistook such forced self-confidence for conceit ? But the victim of so deceptive
an article of faith was really Curzon himself.
For, so strongly did he hold it that, not only was
he the despair of many willing and able secretaries,
who left him because their professional pride
could not stand seeing good work torn up without
any explanation and their Chief's own work
substituted for it ; but also, through his insistence
upon giving close personal attention to every detail
connected with his household arrangements and
his Office, he was invariably overworked and

frequently brought himself to the verge of a nervous
breakdown. During the time that I worked with
him after his return from India, he entrusted me
with the duty of finding house private secretaries
for him. One man (who had an agricultural
degree at Cambridge, was in the University eleven,
a capital rider and a first-rate shot) I snatched
for him—respectfully, I hope!—out of the jaws
of the King of Spain. But he only lasted a few
months, though he was admirably suited for
looking after the farms, managing the horses and
the shooting, etc. etc., for the reasons I have
given. In all I must have engaged six or seven
others : young men of letters, of political ambition
and of full training, but none of them could " stay
the course." The power of delegation was not
included among his gifts, and dearly he paid the
price for missing it.

By reason of this failing and its consequent
effect on his health, many of his friends feared
that he would have to·leave India long before his
first term was up. Will it be easily believed that
this man, when Viceroy, not content with the vast
responsibilities thrown upon his shoulders, made
it his business at Simla to go through every department of every Government office and to become
familiar with its working and acquainted with its
personnel? Here is a quotation from a letter
written to me after his return :

" My conception of the position of Viceroy
was to be head not only of the Government
but of every department of the Government.
. . . The only way to control departments and
to avoid the dangers of a bureaucracy is to
know at least as much as they : grasp of prin-
ciple is not enough ; mastery of detail is essential."

It is not strange that such personal supervision
and examination was not agreeable to the permanent staffs of those offices ; but the desire which
impelled the Viceroy to undertake those duties
might well have been ascribed, even by his enemies,
to motives higher than arrogance and conceit.
Yet I am afraid this passion for efficiency made
many enemies for Curzon during the course of
his official life. I have written elsewhere* that
" he upset the whole *train de vie* of his subordinates,
who never knew when they could get away for
their holidays ; since he insisted that whilst he,
the captain, was on the bridge keeping a sleepless
watch over the ship that he commanded, every
officer under his control should be alert and present
to help him. Many were the complaints laid against
him on the score of over-working a willing staff.
One complaint was never lodged—that he compelled
others to work whilst he idled."

* *Quarterly Review,* July, 1925.

In the foregoing pages I have tried to sketch Curzon in private and in public. There are two other sketches that might be drawn—of Curzon in triumph and in tragedy. The world has been misled by many caricatures of him in triumph ; his tragedy began on leaving India. It deepened soon afterwards on his first wife's death, which darkened his whole outlook on life. Finally it vanished into the night of untold despair when he was denied the office of Prime Minister. Yet, through those last twenty years in shadow, there shone long rays of the old determination to go on working and achieving for the public good. A list of the things that he wrought for Britain between 1905 and 1925 would fill a creditably long index, passing from his epoch-making Chancellorship of Oxford University to many other posts and labours of high responsibility and ending with his tenure of the Foreign Office and his Lord Presidency of the Council. Curzon's was a life of great ambition, great industry, great fulfilment, great disappointment—four acts of a drama threaded together upon the twin cords of patriotic instinct and perpetual pain. It may easily be for physical reasons that, in the last fifteen years of his life, his judgment often failed him, especially in grave crises of internal policy ; his judgment was less sure, and his decisions were less marked and more liable to

change. Herein he often surprised his supporters
and disappointed his friends, losing thereby an
amount of backing which might have stood him
in good stead later on. For, when it was irre-
vocably decided, in 1924, that Mr. Baldwin should
be Prime Minister and not Lord Curzon—a decision
which, as he wrote me, "cut him to the quick," there
was no strong criticism or resentment on public
grounds at the choice then made. But it made
no difference to his behaviour in official life ; he
continued to serve loyally under Baldwin, as he
had served five other Prime Ministers, until the
day of his death.

And this was his goal, as described by his old
friend and political opponent Lord Oxford, in
his funeral oration spoken in the House of Lords
of which Curzon had been the leader :

> " To pursue high ambition by none but
> worthy means, and to take an assured place in
> the long line of those who have enriched by
> their gifts and dignified by their character the
> annals of English public life."

MR. GEORGE WYNDHAM
1863–1913

OF literary and other artistic persons the Mother
of Parliaments has ever been suspicious—though
Canning and Macaulay, Disraeli and John Morley
were among the most distinguished of her sons.
Poets, especially, never appealed to her severely
practical mind. As for " Exquisites "—the Beau
Brummels and Count D'Orsays of England,—she
needed none of these " hues of radiant dawn "
to enhance the glory of her day, and they were
equally averse from wasting their sweetness upon
such desert air. I have known only four men in
the category of " dandies " who were also members
of Parliament: they were " Bobby " (afterwards
Lord) Spencer, Claude Lowther, " Loulou " Harcourt and George Wyndham : the last named was
a poet and an essayist as well. What a combination ;
what a challenge ! But that was exactly what
George Wyndham liked ; he was an Elizabethan
gentleman adventurer, with a dash of the troubadour,
from the crown of his head to the sole of his foot.
Years ago I took him to luncheon in Paris with
Sarah Bernhardt ; instantly she pronounced him
to be the handsomest young man she had ever

seen—and she was no mean judge. A few years later we went together to see Rodin at his studio in the forest of Meudon, and within ten minutes that great sculptor was imploring George to sit for his bust in bronze. With those attractive features, and that form which reminded one of the young Guardsman of legend, went a wonderful expression, a musical voice, the movement of an athlete, and beautiful clothes. He was the perfect specimen of a young, high-spirited English gentleman who could ride to hounds with the best, had fought for his country in the Soudan, and who was known to have literary tastes and an ambition to make his mark in politics. That was the troubadour side of him in his early days, when he flashed into the ken of the House of Commons like a D'Artagnan, and conquered it by his radiance, vitality and charm. Subsequently he added to these qualities a carefully cultivated taste for all things artistic, and became an acknowledged expert in English and French romantic literature, with a decided talent for writing delicate verse and distinguished prose. But George was wise in his generation and well advised, not only by the keen perception of his own family, but also by the prudent counsel of Arthur Balfour, his guide, philosopher, friend and political godfather. He therefore refrained from proclaiming his devotion to the Muses until he had made a host of friends in Parliament

Mr. George Wyndham
in South Africa

and had laid the foundation of a reputation for being a serious student of political affairs.

He did not, however, (nor could he) conceal the adventurous side of his character, which developed quickly when he became private secretary to A.J.B. in Ireland.* Although he had French and Irish blood in him, he was consumed by a passionate love of England and Empire which made him an admirable lieutenant to his intrepid chief. In those gloomy days of political storm on both sides of St. George's Channel, the Home Rule case was being violently advertised by speech and pen, accompanied by daily attacks of the most pernicious kind upon the character of the Chief Secretary, whose head was too full of more important matters for him to pay much attention to such onslaughts. But they could not go by default: so Wyndham was deputed to answer them as they appeared; and a little volume of collected letters, called *Lies and Replies*, shews the zeal and the skill and the knowledge with which he fulfilled his task and which earned for him the genial nickname of "The Smiling Assassin," from the Nationalist party. One could wish that he had preserved that terse, epigrammatic style of expression throughout his public life, especially when in office. But "swerving sickness" overtook him; and he spoiled many good speeches and addresses

* 1889

in later years not only by their inordinate length
but by tricking them out with copious adorn-
ment, flowery metaphor and unnecessary rhetoric—
unusual in a trained writer of almost classical
purity—until he became difficult to follow and
sometimes impossible to listen to. A good story
is told in this connection : George was saying one
day that his beloved sister Pamela had so close a
knowledge of his brain that she perceived what
he meant before he spoke. " Better still," was
the rejoinder of another of her great admirers ;
" she knows what you mean *after* you have spoken."
But this is a digression from my present topic,
which is an appreciation of the devotion and fine
frenzy with which he would throw himself into
any cause which he considered righteous.

There was some surprise and some heart-burning
when it was discovered that, after his hard and
successful work against Mr. Gladstone's Home
Rule Bill, both in Parliament and in the country
(1892–1893), George Wyndham was not to be
included in Lord Salisbury's administration of
1895. But he took it quite serenely, and devoted
himself to literature and sport, with occasional
visits to Westminster, until the Jameson Raid
incident in December, 1895, consequent upon the
alleged ill-treatment of the British population in
the Transvaal. Immediately, George was up in
the saddle again, booted and spurred for the fray,

impelled to battle by his fine Imperial instinct.
South Africa was to him what India had been to
Mr. Disraeli. He wanted to see that sub-continent
" all red " for Britain. Now was his chance, by
avenging the cause of his oppressed fellow-countrymen, to bring about the end which he devoutly
desired. So he organized and spoke and wrote
without ceasing to make the British case known,
not only throughout Great Britain but also in
Canada and in the Antipodes. I saw a great deal
of him during that time, and can bear witness to
the fact that he wore himself to a shadow in this
endeavour, and came close to a nervous breakdown.
That, however, was averted by a visit to South
Africa in July, 1896, to learn all he could at first
hand from Cape Town to Rhodesia before the
threatened explosion occurred. " Thought he was
a Spring poet," said Cecil Rhodes after their
first meeting'; "but he is all chapter and verse."
And so he was, by the time he left that country
to return home; so full of his subject that he was
called in Parliament " the member for South
Africa." On the Parliamentary Commission
appointed to enquire into Dr. Jim's misadventure,
Wyndham was given a place ; not, I imagine, because
he had any claim to impartiality, but to be a make-
weight against men like Harcourt and Labouchere,
who had made no secret of their opinions on the
other side. Still, for all his known bias, George

played the game as a Commissioner should, and
earned the praise, in private, of both the men
I have named for his conduct during the proceedings. Then followed the South African War,
during the first half of which he was Under Secretary
at the War Office, and reached the acme of his
fame as a parliamentary speaker and as a champion
of the British Army which, little prepared for an
over-seas campaign of such magnitude, was passing
through the " Valley of the shadow " in defence
of the British Empire in the dark days of December,
1899. The Imperialist, the soldier, the adventurer; in a word the real, mature George Wyndham,
showed to splendid advantage during the whole
of that period, and proved himself worthy of promotion in 1900 to the responsible office of Chief
Secretary for Ireland.

There I was privileged to join him as his parliamentary private secretary; and a more attractive
chief it is impossible to conceive. His power of
work was prodigious. Nobody who was not
close to him can imagine how much he put into
the day: beginning (in the summer months) at
7 a.m. with lawn tennis or riding or running in
the Phœnix Park to keep himself fit ; then a hurried
breakfast; then dashing off to his office at the
Castle till six o'clock, with a break for luncheon
at the Kildare Street Club. Then back again to
the Chief Secretary's Lodge (always driving past

the grim scene of poor Lord Frederick Cavendish's murder), where London letters had to be answered and newspapers read until dinner time either at home or abroad. Dinner was always festive and interesting wherever he was. Like the Irish themselves, he believed that the distressful country could " only be governed by conversation and arbitary decisions " and we were lucky if the conversations ceased before 2 a.m. I felt at the time, as did many others, that if there had been less conversation and more decision it might have been better in the end both for Wyndham and his province. But he certainly impressed upon priests and farmers and peasants alike that he was indeed their Haroun al Raschid (as he once described himself), with gifts for the asking if they in return gave him their whole confidence. But, unfortunately, that is not in the power of the Irishman to give, even to his neighbour ; and certainly not to a British official of whom, however charming, he has a traditional suspicion. Wyndham, however, was as good as his word and, trusting them as he believed they trusted him, he cajoled the British Treasury into providing piers and harbours, money for fisheries and I know not what else, to make life in the poorer areas more endurable ; and he crowned these acts of beneficence with his Land Act which still stands as a monument to his industry, parliamentary skill, and affection for the

Irish people. So popular did he, apparently
become; so pleased and grateful when all men
spoke well of him, that he quickened his pace
without noticing that his direction had changed.
Imperceptibly to himself he was being led, by men
whose " conversation " had a double meaning,
to listen to counsel that headed straight towards
a change in the political status of Ireland ; a change
which was anathema to Ulster and foreign to the
British conception of a " United " Kingdom. Thus
came about his downfall and resignation from
the Government, due largely to his quixotic
loyalty in declining to dismiss a subordinate and
to betray a friend who had grievously misled
him. Long afterwards he said to me, " I see Politics
by the light of Art " ; but, alas, we know the
fate of many fine artists whose generous impulses
have caused them to forget that we must curb
our imaginations on the rein of practical common-
sense. George was never practical; he was too
generous, too adventurous, too much in a hurry
to see the Millennium. O the pity of it ! If his
heart had not been wrapped up in the prosperity
of Ireland, he could have had promotion to higher
offices two years before he fell. He has written :

" It is a curious development that, with
Exchequer, Colonies and War Office vacant,
I should feel it an absolute duty to stay here

(in Ireland) . . . . If I deserted them now, all
the work since A.J.B. in '87 to '91 would be
imperilled. . . . They do still, in fact, believe
in me."

Therefore I insist that, so far as George was concerned, his catastrophe was rooted in the selfless
and single-hearted belief, however mistaken, that
the policy which he was pursuing was for the
ultimate good of Ireland and one which, no matter
at what cost of self-sacrifice, he was determined
to follow to the end. So do not judge him too
hardly ; at the worst he had misread the function
of the political machine (the House of Commons
majority) which alone could manufacture his
theory into a practical result ; he got entangled
in it and was broken on its wheel.

But of such fine stuff was he that, after the
General Election of 1906, when the fortunes of
the Unionist party were at their lowest, he flung
himself once more into the battle : for Religious
Education, for Tariff Reform, and in defence of
the House of Lords, with a faith and an enthusiasm which regained for him all, or more than
all, he had lost in public confidence. His loyalty
and courage had rallied his friends, and they
were legion ; his indomitable energy in supporting
every Imperial movement took him as a welcome
guest to platforms all over the country ; his love

of adventure and his accessibility lent a willing ear to new causes in search of a champion with a ready blade. How much more might he have done for his country if his life had been spared to her for the normal span of years—this gallant gentleman whose inspiration was Disraeli, whose example was Mr. Balfour, whose ideals were pure and beyond challenge? It is but empty speculation to pursue such a question. *Felix opportunitate mortis* or otherwise, he has left a splendid memory behind him among those for whom and with whom he worked; the memory of a man of high courage in politics and of high culture in letters, with the Elizabethan spirit and a heart of gold.

MR. ALFRED LYTTELTON

1857–1913

WHEN Arthur Benson first saw Alfred Lyttelton at Eton he described him as " a big boy clothed with unapproachable glory; the undisputed King of the place." The House of Commons is a very different place from any public school; there the finest of international athletes or the most popular of men, in whatever sphere of social activity, joins the parliamentary family-circle on terms of absolute equality with the Board-school boy and the recluse and the fellow who never won a prize for athletics in his life. Some move up, some move down, in general esteem; but " previous performances " outside the world of politics are of little or no account at Westminster unless a man can make good, in one way or another, within the walls of Parliament itself. So that Alfred, with all his brilliant record behind him, started his political career in 1895 much like the rest of us; but, as he had already done in other fields of fame, he soon left us far behind.

There was no little curiosity to see him—this public figure, this popular favourite—as he came forward to take the oath of allegiance as a new

boy to a new school. How would he deport
himself, this household-name in the cricket world
of the last twenty years, this amateur champion
at racquets and at real tennis, this rising barrister
of thirty-eight years old who had already begun
to score in the Law Courts? But curiosity was
soon satisfied. Alfred belonged already to a family
with a genius for knowing the rules and the tradi-
tions and the technique of every game as soon as
they saw it played; and he slipped into the game
of politics as though he had played it all his life.
He came and saw and conquered.

That Parliament of 1895 contained a large sprink-
ling of Eton and Cambridge men to whom Alfred
was already a hero. The older ones had known
him as a dashing international football player and
captain of the Eton and Cambridge elevens in
the 'seventies. Had he not been chosen for the
Gentlemen v. Players before he was twenty, and
for England against Australia before he was
twenty-one? Oxford sighed to think that, if
Alfred had had his way, he might have gone up
to University College to read history, instead of
to Trinity, Cambridge; and that the lustre of his
fame might have added brilliance to the athletic
glories of the City of Spires. But this was not
to be; family tradition was not to be denied, and
one of Alfred's consolations (in his own words) was
that at any rate he would not have to play against his

MR. ALFRED LYTTELTON
Brighton, 1893

brother Edward in the University match at Lord's.
" It was horrible to think of," he wrote, when the
decision was finally made. The younger M.P.'s who
were to be his colleagues for the next twenty years
had heard of his prowess at Eton and Cambridge,
and had looked upon him in their boyhood as upon a
demi-god, with eyes of veneration when he revisited
his old haunts to play a match in Upper Club or
at Fenner's whilst they were still *in statu pupillari*.
From all of these Alfred could be sure of a warm
welcome in the House of Commons, as also from
the members in the legal profession in which he
was already making a considerable name.   This
was a good start ; the rest depended upon himself.

I am very conscious of the risk of attempting
to give a true idea of any man nearly twenty
years after his death.   Especially is this dangerous
where Alfred is concerned ; for one retains old
memories of him which, as of rare wine, are
likely to be exaggerated in praise when one revives
the story of past excellence, even of hero-worship.
So I am fortunate in discovering that, in the year
of his death, I wrote a short impression of him
which appeared in his Biography, published by
his wife in 1917.   This is what I felt about him
then, and what I still feel :

" Somehow I always think of Alfred in the
House of Commons more as an atmosphere than

as a parliamentarian. From the first day of his
arrival the House 'was glad of him.' Until he
became Colonial Secretary he spoke very little,
but his fellowship was felt all the time. All sorts
and conditions of men consulted him, and nobody
that I ever heard of sought his advice in vain.
In politics, as in everything else, he was sporting
and fair and reasonable. He had an ingrained
sense of 'the rules of the game,' and, whatever
the provocation, he was no more capable of
taking an unfair advantage of his opponents than
he was of disputing the umpire's decision at Lord's.
He did not need to prove all this : everybody
knew it about him from the first ; but there were
some who misunderstood him and thought that
he might have served his cause better if he had
been more uncompromising in manner and less
suave in speech. But they were wrong. He
was in the Cabinet in days when Party feeling ran
at its highest, and when the Colonial Office was
the perpetual target of slings and arrows that no
man could number. But Alfred's temper never
failed him ; his judgment never swerved : and in
all the fierce controversies that succeeded the
South African War, and in all the domestic struggles
over Tariff Reform which hampered the Unionist
party's usefulness for so long, he stood high among
those few who, though in the forefront of the battle,
never lost a friend."

Yes : I still think that it was the atmosphere of Alfred that counted for most in his day and generation. He was brought up in the heart of a deeply Christian family where piety was as natural as priggishness was abhorred. Those who never knew him can read in his published letters, and his friends do not need to be reminded, how much his religion meant to Alfred, nor how richly it coloured the background of his character from his Eton days until the end of his life. It kept him smiling and serene *in arduis rebus* ; it heightened his reverence for people and for things ; it upheld and steadied him in the dark days of bereavement ; perhaps it had something to do with the sensible gaiety and *joie de vivre* which radiated from his personality wherever it went. " He is like a running stream with the sun on it," wrote his Eton tutor ; " he is the champagne of cricket," said old W. G. Grace in his prime. That affectionate greeting to men and women alike ; that sunny smile, that infectious shout of enthusiasm, that intuitive sympathy for all his fellow-creatures ; who that knew him does not remember a score of instances of these endearing qualities ? Alfred was a supreme influence for good ; and it penetrated into a great many strata of our national life, the more deeply because he was wholly unconscious of it.

He was not a great speaker either at the Bar

or in the House of Commons; but he was a very
good one. His genius seemed to lie less in the
direction of advocacy than of arbitration, for he
cared more for justice than for victory. And full
advantage was taken of this rare quality of mind
by the British Government of the day, which
despatched him in 1900 to South Africa, and to
Newfoundland two years later, to decide upon
claims and compensations that he adjusted with
a minimum of friction, thanks to his gentle candour
of language, firmness of purpose, and above all
to that indefinable quality called " charm " with
which his personality had been so lavishly endowed.

I think that, far more than any of his brothers,
Alfred valued and cultivated the friendship and
acquaintance of people of all ages and of all classes.
Somebody said of him that he was " the natural
friend of all generations." I remember once
meeting him at Eton when he was surrounded by
a group of boys in the School Yard, and afterwards
walking down the High Street with him and
noticing how many young Etonians he greeted
by name.

" What an extraordinary number of boys
you seem to know, Alfred," I said to him.

" I do," he replied. " But you must remember, *I have been here three days.*"

And so it was with the masters at Eton, with
dons and undergraduates at Cambridge; even

when we were yachting together round Sicily, he made friends with sailors and peasants and artists wherever we put into port. Like his life-long friend, Arthur Balfour, he had a strange curiosity to know all that could be known about human nature from personal experience; and his tastes, even more varied than those of A.J.B., enabled him to gratify that curiosity to an almost unlimited extent. For he was, without being too much of a scholar, an enthusiastic lover of literature and enjoyed the society of men of letters; his enthusiasm for good music knew no bounds —it did not matter whether we were singing madrigals or more difficult works in the old " Magpies " society under Lionel Benson, or in the Bach Choir; or whether he was listening entranced to something far greater at a Leeds Festival.

He was a keen rider to hounds, so long as the funds held out, and I daresay he knew all of the hounds by name. A beautiful shot, too, whose style was an example for every young man to copy and whose generous appreciation of a good day's sport (whether much or little was killed) was the joy of every keeper and beater on the ground. But equally well he knew the work of the Cambridge Mission in South London and the needs of the people that it lived to serve. That knowledge it was, perhaps, that stimulated him

L

to interest himself in Housing and Temperance questions, with which he was so closely identified in later life, and which brought him into more than brotherly touch with all sorts and conditions of men. His was the catholic-complex that made him " the natural friend of all generations."

But now, back to Alfred in Parliament : the well-dressed gentleman, the loose-limbed athlete, the lean and clean-shaved barrister with the friendly disarming smile. I remember, as if it were yesterday, the personal success of one of his first speeches, when he moved the Address to the Throne in 1897. I can see him now, in his black velvet Court suit, perfectly at ease as though he were facing Spofforth at the Oval; speaking as naturally, on that particularly artificial occasion, as a man who might be having an engrossing conversation with a cultivated friend in the smoking-room. No effort, no indecision, free delivery, graceful English—*style*. It was an immediate success. Not long after that, the Boer War broke out and, as I have said, he was sent as Chairman of a Commission to South Africa, where he was so successful that Lord Milner hoped that a second Alfred might succeed him as High Commissioner. Instead of which, he succeeded Mr. Chamberlain as Colonial Secretary and inherited all the responsibilities of the aftermath of the South African War. He had to face the bitterest opposition to the " Lyttelton Con-

stitution," a scheme which he had invented to
bridge over the interim until self-government
could be granted to South Africa ; he had to bear
the brunt of vehement hostility to the importation
of Chinese labour to carry on work in the South
African mines—" Chinese Slavery " was the Liberal
slogan to victory in the General Election of 1906
—and he was the central figure in a now forgotten
but then hideous episode at the height of an
embittered debate on Tariffs in 1905 when, for a
full hour, he stood at the box to speak, but was
prevented from so doing by the deplorable clamour
of a united Liberal and Irish opposition.   Heaven
forbid that, in writing about Alfred, I should
revive any memories of that humiliating night—
but one ; none of us who were present will ever
forget the patience, the courage and the exasper-
ating good-humour with which he faced that den of
roaring lions and came through the ordeal unscathed.
When he accepted, very diffidently, the high
office of Colonial Secretary we had triumphed in
our hero's crown of glory ; but it was a crown of
thorns.

In the General Election of 1906, Alfred Lyttelton,
like Arthur Balfour and many others, lost his seat,
but was returned soon afterwards at a by-election
for St. George's, Hanover Square.   Then came,
at last, the long pent-up fundamental battles
between the victorious Liberals and the vanquished

Conservatives upon essential questions : such as Religious Education, Welsh Disestablishment, " advanced " Liberal Budgets and the existence of the House of Lords. In all of these grave matters of dispute Alfred Lyttelton fought for his side with all the strength of his conscience and conviction, but with a weary heart. Despair was not a word included in his vocabulary ; but the light of the joy of battle was no longer in his eyes, and many of us thought that he would be happier, after all, if he could find some outlet for his abounding health and energy in spheres unconnected with the clash of party strife. Suddenly, the end came. He had just returned from a delightful journey to East Africa ; he had made first-rate speeches against Home Rule and Welsh Disestablishment ; he went down to play in a local cricket match at Bethnal Green where he made eighty-nine runs. That was his last innings. He had been hit by a rising ball in some vulnerable spot. He did not feel or know the extent of the damage ; but a few days afterwards his obituary notice appeared in *The Times*.

To his friends of my generation and of its predecessor, it was as though there had been an eclipse of the sun. I cannot describe the feeling ; it was shared by the whole House of Commons, by the Bar, and by countless hosts of known and unknown friends. He was buried at his home

at Hagley on July 8th, 1913, whilst the Oxford
and Cambridge match was being played at Lord's.
At the hour of his funeral the great game, of which
he had been so brilliant and popular an exponent,
was interrupted : the pavilion flags were lowered ;
all the players and the vast concourse of spectators rose and stood with bared heads, in respectful
mourning for him who knew, and by his example
had taught others in every department of life,
how to " play the game."

OTHER FORE-MEN

(UNIONISTS)

In the foregoing chapters I have tried to draw sketches of a few of the Prime Ministers and their lieutenants with whom I was brought into contact during my service at Westminster. But there were others, many others, of no less eminence in public life than some of those whom I have sketched because I felt that I knew them better.

SIR MICHAEL HICKS-BEACH*

1834–1916

Such an one, for example, was Sir Michael Hicks-Beach who entered Parliament in 1864 and sat upon the Treasury Bench four years later. A tall, aristocratic figure with a well-trimmed beard, partly concealing a firm and thin-lipped mouth ; we were rather afraid of him. He was an out-and-out party man, a Tory of the Tories, a stern disciplinarian, who had learned his politics under Mr. Disraeli and knew what party loyalty meant. His programme was a rigid one, graven on his conscience and as enduring as the Ten Command-

* Created Earl St. Aldwyn, 1906.

ments : it included religious education, for he was
a pillar of the Established Church, free-trade and
relentless financial economy. For the rest, he was
a country gentleman of the old breed who disliked
London, was reserved with his colleagues unless
he was fighting them, and was a staunch believer
in the patriotic slogan " My country, right or
wrong."   Black Michael, as he was generally
known, was a great Chancellor of the Exchequer
who had an admirable way with him when he was
on his feet in the House of Commons. Suave and
dexterous in debate, lucid in statement, the Bill
that was in his charge was pretty sure of getting
through. But " off the bench " he was not at all
an accessible Minister, uncertain of temper and
possessed of a tongue that it was difficult to control.
Most of us who were private secretaries working
for other Ministers came under its lash sooner
or later, and we did not go out of our way to
repeat the experience more often than was necessary.
But he was one of those public men whom England
likes and, though neither his temperament nor
his health would have made him a successful leader
of the party, he was a man whom everybody
trusted.

MR. WALTER LONG*

1854–1924

WALTER LONG, of quite a different fibre, was just
such another. He, too, was a plain blunt man,
very irascible at times and took no pains to disguise the fact. But nobody thought the worse
of him for that; his gusts of temper passed as
quickly as clouds across the sun; and when they
had vanished, we saw a shining bald head being
mopped by a large red bandanna handkerchief and
a face that beamed as though he had not an antagonist in the House. He was a model of the old-
fashioned fox-hunting squire of broad acres in
Wiltshire, who loved his country and his home,
his tenants, his horses, and his glass of port. What
he did not know about Agriculture and Local
Government from personal experience was not
worth knowing, and the Government offices that
deal with these intricate subjects were never
better managed than during the years when he
presided over them. And this knowledge stood
him in good stead when he went over to Ireland
to succeed George Wyndham as Chief Secretary
—but a very different person from his predecessor
with his Celtic impulses and his passion to please
everybody. Only one thing they had in common,

* Created Viscount Long of Wraxhall, 1921.

VISCOUNT LONG

[*Sport and General*

and that was their delight in riding a good horse across good country. Walter Long was English to the backbone, with fixed opinions upon the principles of government which nothing could change and no environment could modify. He was a man of immense courage and was never afraid of letting his opinions be known ; his reward was that he was a real success in Ireland and genuinely popular wherever he went.

Many of his parliamentary friends would have liked him to follow Mr. Balfour as leader of the Unionist Party, but I have never felt quite sure that he would have proved equal to the task. If honesty, plain speaking and hard work were the only qualities necessary in a leader, we could not have chosen a better man than Walter Long. But there are other gifts at least as necessary as these ; wide vision, imagination, dexterity in debate, and a certain serenity (whether natural or affected) which he could not always command. So he and his friendly rival, Mr. Austen Chamberlain, both made way for Bonar Law ; an imperfect solution of a perplexing situation, where both men had about an equal number of supporters, but perhaps the wisest solution under the circumstances. Like Sir Michael Hicks-Beach, he was a splendid party man and, though passed over for the leadership, he gave his unfaltering and enthusiastic support to " Bonar " who had been preferred before him. I used to see a great deal of him in connection with the Union Defence League between the years 1906 and 1910 when Mr. Birrell was governing Ireland, and a better chief never walked the floor of a Government office. But I believe that after all is said and done, and after full account has been rendered of all his services to the country at the Admiralty, in Ireland and elsewhere, the most courageous and splendid thing that he did in his official life was to pass the Dog Muzzling Act, in the teeth of violent opposition from all parties and from both sexes, and so to free England from the scourge of hydrophobia for the last thirty years.

MR HENRY CHAPLIN*

1840–1923

AND then "the Squire," as Mr. Harry Chaplin was affectionately known on every race-course and at every farmer's "ordinary" throughout the land. The very sight of that dignified and portly figure buttoned into a very tight frock-coat, wearing a rather curly-brimmed silk hat tilted over his eyes as he sat on the Front Bench, made you think at once of Hermit and Corn Laws and the Coaching Club, of Regency bucks and cambric

* Created Viscount Chaplin, 1916

Viscount Chaplin

stocks and quizzing-glasses. Henry Chaplin
was a great survival of those spacious days, and
not only in appearance. Nature had certainly
intended him to be born during the period when
the great territorial families ruled England, and
ruled her very well; when there was no " Black
Country " and the landed gentry went up to Parliament, as in duty bound, to make the laws for the
land and made very good ones on the whole.
Dignity and decorum, in deportment and in debate,
were innate in him. Turbulence and " scenes in
the House " were anathema, and he turned from
them in disgust. He was a very good attendant
at Westminster, both in and out of office, when
the claims of Doncaster or the " Royal " were
not too insistent : sitting for hours in his place
with a sheet of foolscap in his hand and apparently
making copious notes for an impending speech
(as the Press fondly imagined) but in reality drawing
sketches of horses all over the paper. The " Squire "
was a speaker of amazing, almost fatal, fluency,
who had trained himself so to follow current
events that he could " intervene " whenever
required to reply to an opponent or to " talk out "
a debate on any conceivable subject. He thoroughly
enjoyed speaking; his manner was in the grand
manner and, when he began to address the House,
you got the impression of a Roman Emperor
about to make a great and benevolent oration to

his people. He rose from his seat with fine deliberation and placed his hat carefully beside the
sacred box. There he stood for a moment surveying
the scene; you remarked the profusion of his
chestnut locks and of the white pocket handkerchief that flowed from the breast-pocket of his
coat. He screwed his monocle into its place and
you were struck by the smallness of his eyes and
of his mouth. The scene was set, the central
figure was set, and the speech began very quietly,
according to the established rules of classic oratory.
Onward it rolled and rolled, with varying tones,
pauses and gestures all complete: rhetorical,
sometimes redundant, courteous always though a
little pained by interruptions or impatience; but
generally much too long for a generation that
had outgrown the adage that " speech was given
us to conceal our thoughts," and which no longer
cared for Corinthian decoration on the pillars of
the State. But he was so genial a personality,
such a general favourite, that all these weaknesses
were easily forgiven him by his audience, though
less easily by those who moved restlessly in their
places for hours in the hope of catching the Speaker's
eye when ' Mr. Harry ' had resumed his seat. On
the platform in the country, and especially at a
meeting in an agricultural constituency, the Squire
was a great draw. Time was of less importance
there, and he was universally popular; the people

began their cheers of welcome when they saw the
arrival of the pint bottle of champagne carefully
placed on the table to await him ; they applauded
his speech from beginning to end, reserving a
special salvo for the moment when, at the conclusion of his oration, the hero of the evening
produced a silver flask and refreshed himself with
a long draught of its contents.

It was a bitter day for him when, after his long
Front Bench service extending over thirty years,
he found that he was not included in Mr. Balfour's
Ministry of 1903. No wonder that he " supposed
Arthur had made a mistake ", and that it would
be put right in a day or two. But alas, the mistake
was never discovered, and the Squire departed
to the third bench below the gangway—just as
he saw the dawn of Protection, of whose coming
he had been the faithful herald for forty years,
rising not in the Eastern Counties but in Birmingham. He took with him, into his official retirement,
the hearty sympathy of the whole country ; and
his elevation to the House of Lords was received
with general delight. No wonder he was popular ;
for he was such a fine old English gentleman,
so urbane, so friendly, such a sportsman. I owe
him a great deal. Before presenting myself as
Conservative candidate for a Suffolk seat, I asked
him for an interview to discuss my chances. He
had never heard of me and I had never met him,

so I was extremely nervous as to the reception that might await me. Moreover, we were to meet at 10.30 a.m., rather an early hour for a man of the Squire's habits. However, I presented myself at his door in Berkeley Square and was shown into a delightful drawing-room. After a short wait, an elderly butler passed solemnly down the room, bearing a silver breakfast set with which he disappeared through folding doors. Another quarter of an hour passed, and I was becoming more and more nervous, when the doors were thrown open and there appeared this tall, dignified figure, partially attired and clad in a flowered silk dressing-gown. He might have stepped right out of an eighteenth-century picture frame. Nobody could have been kinder to me than he was; I might have known him from boyhood. He provided me with all the information for which I asked; gave me admirable political advice which I never forgot and tried to follow and, finally, promised to do all he could to help me into Parliament. And in the same way I know that he assisted many others. Accessibility is a cardinal virtue in statesmen who have " arrived." Young men never forget their kindness.

MR. GOSCHEN*

1831–1907

FOR Mr. Goschen, another of the big figures of
the day on the Conservative side, we all had the
greatest regard. It was an honour to sit in the
same House, in 1895, and upon the same side of it,
with the venerable statesman who had been an
M.P. since the days of Lord Palmerston, had held
Cabinet office as long ago as 1866, and had been
First Lord of the Admiralty under Mr. Gladstone
in 1871. Without being a quite first-rate scholar,
he had a very distinguished career both at Rugby
and at Oriel College, Oxford, of which University
he subsequently became Chancellor on the death
of Lord Salisbury. His public life began in the
City of London, and so highly was he considered
that in 1858, at the age of twenty-nine, he was
made a Director of the Bank of England, and
was elected soon afterwards as one of the Members
for the City. In his knowledge of the politics
of finance he was scarcely second to Mr. Gladstone
himself, and greatly his superior in his grasp of
foreign affairs. It was, I believe, really because
he could not follow his Chief whole-heartedly
along the path of non-Imperial, non-intervention
policy that he declined to take office in 1880,

* Created Viscount Goschen, 1900.

though the reason assigned was a different one ; thus he kept himself free to play the part of a determined critic of the Administration which governed the country through those fateful five years and shattered the confidence of the nation in the Liberal party for the best part of a generation. Goschen once described himself as a violent man of moderate views, and he was not wide of the mark ; for with such vehemence of language did he denounce the extreme policies of Mr. Gladstone both at home and abroad, that it became obvious, even before the introduction of the first Home Rule Bill, that he and Mr. Gladstone could never sit in the same Cabinet again.   He always belonged to the right wing of the Liberal party, so that he had no long road to travel before he found himself in general accord with the Conservatives.   He was the first of the Liberal Unionists to join Lord Salisbury's Government, in succession to Lord Randolph Churchill, who had negligently "forgotten Goschen" when (believing himself to be indispensable) he suddenly resigned the office of Chancellor of the Exchequer in 1886.   High feeling ran through the ranks of the Conservative party at that time, and it was reported that Goschen declined to purchase Lord Randolph's official robes from him.   Where-upon the out-going Chancellor remarked with some asperity, "I should have thought Goschen would be the last man to refuse to buy ' old clothes.' "

He was a powerful accretion of strength to Lord
Salisbury's Administration. In addition to his
immense responsibilities as Chancellor, he constantly found himself bearing the burden of Leader
of the House of Commons during the enforced
absences of Mr. W. H. Smith, who was then
First Lord of the Treasury; and with so much
acceptance did he fulfil this task that, on the death
of Mr. Smith in 1891, if capacity and experience
had been the only qualities necessary, Goschen
would certainly have been his successor. But,
unfortunately for him perhaps, he was then a
Liberal Unionist, not a Conservative; and the
" usual channels " conveyed to Lord Salisbury the
definite opinion of the Conservative party that,
though they admired and appreciated Mr. Goschen
without reservation, they would prefer the leadership of the House of Commons to be entrusted
to a Conservative. So Mr. Balfour was chosen
in his stead. It was the willing price that Goschen
paid for changing his allegiance, for revising his
principles; and if anyone cares to find a great
example of political understanding and personal
generosity, he should read the published correspondence in which Lord Salisbury regretted that he
could not offer the post of First Lord to Goschen,
and in which the latter accepted the decision with
a loyalty that almost amounted to enthusiasm.
There were not wanting those who charged him,

M

as they charged Mr. Chamberlain a few years later, with motives of personal ambition to account for his change of party, and who upbraided him for his apparent lack of consistency. Such accusations left his withers unwrung. Goschen was no slave to any prejudice or obsession; his intellect guided his conscience in all that he did from his earliest days. Even as an undergraduate, when President of the Oxford Union, he expressed strong views on the risk of worshipping consistency as an idol!

"Consistency is not the highest form of virtue nor is inconsistency one of the worst forms of crime. To lay too much stress on it is infinitely dangerous. It is to hold out inducements to men to continue in error after they have discovered it; to lend a deaf ear to argument lest their convictions, which they are bound never to alter, should receive a shock."

This short homily is worthy of consideration by men of all parties to-day when everything around us, except shibboleths, seems to be changing for better or for worse.

I had known Mr. Goschen slightly before I became an M.P., when I was a young attaché in Berlin, whither he came on some official business. He was a big, rugged, stooping man, rather Jewish in appearance, terribly short-sighted, with a husky

VISCOUNT GOSCHEN

voice and a delightful sense of humour ; an excellent
German scholar, a cultured man of letters, and
also a very good critic of the theatre, about which
he knew more than most men. And he was a
real orator, combining eloquence and enthusiasm,
who could hold large audiences spell-bound,
whether in Parliament or in the country, for as
long as he cared to speak. I first heard him in
Edinburgh at a great meeting which he and Lord
Hartington were addressing soon after they seceded
from Mr. Gladstone's party ; and, boy though I
was at the time, I have never forgotten the telling
phrase that he used—referring to the courage of
the Irish Loyalists, who would never surrender to
the tyranny of crime that stalked unchecked through
Ireland at that time : " They will make their wills
and do their duty." In debate he was formidable,
never missing a point and capable of a crushing
reply. I was always told that he was quite as
fine an administrator at the Treasury or the
Admiralty as he was a parliamentarian ; and I know
that both Lord Salisbury and Mr. Balfour had the
greatest faith in his judgment.

LORD HALSBURY

1823–1921

AND there are many others whose outstanding
personalities cross the threshold of my memory as

I try to gather into a single picture my impressions of the statesmen of the Conservative party who have passed to their rest. There is the considerable, though faintly comic, figure of Lord Halsbury, who for so many years was Lord Chancellor of England and, to the end of his life, a Die-Hard and a Tory of the Tories : a brilliant advocate and very learned in the law; an incisive orator who revelled in hard language with the same youthful exuberance as Mr. Lloyd-George, and one who presided over the House of Lords with a dignity that was all his own. On the Woolsack, in his robes, he would have made an admirable subject for a " Toby Jug ; " so plump was he, with a round ruddy face that betrayed his irrepressible good-humour. He always looked as though he had lived his long life on old port and high Tory principles. I do not know about the first of these ; but, as regards the second, I am perfectly sure that no man whom I have ever met in high respon-sible position was a more perfect embodiment of " Fear God, Honour the King, Obey the Law and ' Damn the Consequences '."

LORD MILNER

1854–1925

WHICH brings me by an easy transition, for those who remember his famous phrase, to Lord Milner ;

VISCOUNT MILNER

a great pro-Consul who, after a long and successful
career as a Civil Servant, passed to the House of
Lords and became a Cabinet Minister. He was of
the Goschen type, with German blood (I think)
in his veins. A man of wide education and culture,
slow to form an opinion and then rigid in main-
taining it ; at first a little bureaucratic, perhaps,
in his outlook on politics but, later in life, inspired
by the widest Imperialistic vision and utterly
courageous. He was a quite unflinching man and,
to those who did not know him intimately, he
made no great appeal. But to others, to those
few choice and brilliant spirits who worked with
and for him in South Africa, he was their hero
" *sans peur et sans reproche*." The England of
to-day, the British Empire of to-day, appreciate
all too little of what they owe to the head of what
once was known as " Milner's Kindergarten " in
South Africa, a sodality of young men of unusual
intellectual attainments, high enthusiasms and
clear vision, whom he trained to be worthy of and
to hold some of the most responsible posts in our
Empire. The history of our time will not say of
Milner, with his rather frigid exterior, his unpre-
possessing oratory, and with his almost disdainful
attitude toward popular sentiment and opinion,
that he was a tower of strength to his party in
Parliament. He entered the political arena too
late in life to assimilate those tricks of the trade

that make of their possessors popular favourites ; nor do I think that he had the least ambition to master them. But he had other qualities far transcending these talents in permanent worth : he had loyalty and courage, and an illimitable faith in the destiny of the British Empire as a dynamic factor to speed the progress of civilisation and to ameliorate the common lot of the human race.

LORD BALFOUR OF BURLEIGH

1849–1921

THEN Lord Balfour of Burleigh : a huge, solid Scotsman, standing " six feet four in his stocking feet " as his countrymen would say, and burly in every sense of the word. He was a typical Scottish laird, who devoted his life to public work and to the care of his tenantry by whom he was beloved. What he did not know about Scottish affairs, social, agricultural and ecclesiastical, was insignificant—a training which made him an admirable Secretary of State for Scotland. But his principal, and perhaps his best, work was done as Chairman of Committee in the House of Lords, and as an arbitrator in many difficult cases of great importance where his clear, calm judgment, his power of quick decision, his courtesy and absolute impartiality had full scope and were appreciated by all who came in contact with him.

On the platform he was an excellent and popular
speaker ; in the field a brilliant, if sometimes rather
a jealous shot ; in the club or at dinner, a delightful
companion, with a fine sense of humour and an
inexhaustible fund of Scottish stories which he
told with the skill of an artist. " B. of B.," as he
was generally known, was no " limelight " man ;
but rather one of those who preferred to keep
his left hand in ignorance of what his right hand
was doing. And the great things that he succeeded
in doing—and the fusion of the Scottish Churches
is one of those things for which he wrought—are
gratefully treasured in the memories of his fellow-
countrymen.

LORD LONDONDERRY
1852–1915

LORD LONDONDERRY, another great public servant,
was a man who, if he had chosen to do so, could
have lived a long life in idle luxury to the end of
his days. But, instead of so doing, he employed
his wealth to spread happiness among all classes
of the community, and especially among those
dependent upon him in his great estates in the
North of England and in Ireland ; his hospitality
was unbounded, and was dispensed with a natural
charm and gaiety of manner which made of him
a very prince of hosts. For him public life was

a duty incumbent upon him to discharge in return
for the high position and the fortune which he
had inherited; and, whether as Viceroy in Ireland
or in Cabinet office, he worked as hard as any man
for the good of his country and the success of the
Conservative cause. His friends were legion in
both camps; and his London house was, as it
still is, at the disposal of his political chiefs for
conferences or receptions, as well as for the
promotion of all worthy causes. He was " hail
fellow, well met " with everybody, old or young,
in any walk of life, and he radiated happiness
wherever he went, speaking or racing, hunting or
shooting. When I hear the prevalent loose talk
about the hoarding and misuse of wealth, especially
in the hands of Peers, my mind goes back to the
open-hearted generosity and public spirit of Lord
Londonderry, and of many others like him, who
of their own free will devoted life and money
to the good of all classes of the community.

LORD GEORGE HAMILTON
1845–1927

LORD GEORGE HAMILTON was another of the " Old
Guard " who entered Parliament under the auspices
of Mr. Disraeli, with whom he was a prime favourite,
in the year 1868. And there he sat, on the Front
Bench from 1874, in office and out of office, until

1905. During that time he proved himself first of all a good election fighter, under stormier conditions than the present, with an elegant presence and a ready wit which readily ingratiated him with his fellow-members and assisted him to lead many a light cavalry sortie in support of his party in the House. He was always something of a puzzle to me, but no doubt this was due to my own lack of perspicacity. He had occupied a number of important posts in Government to the complete satisfaction of all his chiefs and— this is quite as necessary—enjoying the full confidence of his departmental subordinates who felt that they were not only his colleagues but his friends. He was a most competent administrator, both at the Admiralty and the India Office. Yet in Parliament one got the impression that he was of lighter metal than most of his colleagues in Cabinet; and his nervous, hurried way of speaking made it difficult for him to " hold " the House. He was not quite so accessible as some others to younger members, nor to the new ideas which were always permeating the Conservative party; and he was sadly resentful if they, sometimes his own relatives, pointed out what they conceived to be a better way. So bound up was he, by temperament and tradition, with the earlier party programmes that, like Lord Balfour of Burleigh and Lord Londonderry and others, he found it difficult either to follow Mr. Chamberlain on the Tariff question or to throw in his lot whole-heartedly with Mr. Balfour. So, having resigned Cabinet office in 1903, he retired from Parliament two years later, and Westminster saw him no more. But his public spirit and wide administrative experience were still, fortunately, at the disposal of the Government of the day which turned his happy talents to the best advantage by appointing him Chairman of the important Royal Commission to enquire into the Poor Law and Unemployment, a body which was in session from 1905 until 1909; and then by nominating him, in 1917, to preside over the Mesopotamian Commission which sat during the Great War.

SIR EDWARD CLARKE

1841–1931

I THOUGHT that I had written the last of these brief sketches when the sad news reached me of the death of a very old friend, Sir Edward Clarke, at the ripe age of ninety. It would have been impossible to write of some of those who were foremost in the parliamentary fray during my apprenticeship at Westminster without mention of him. Few men of my time combined to so high a degree the talents that make a reputation both in the Law Courts and in the House of Commons.

He has told us himself something of his romantic history, which began in very humble circumstances and led him to great fame as a barrister and to Government office in Lord Salisbury's Administration in 1886. I think that the first time I heard him speak, in that quiet and earnest voice, was in 1893 when he was chosen by his party to reply to Mr. Gladstone when he introduced the second Home Rule Bill. It was a magnificent performance which, with its immediate grasp of outline and detail, could only have been undertaken by a man of brilliant legal training and experience. There he stood, faced by an eager and enthusiastic crowd of followers of the Parliamentary giant who had just sat down amid tumultuous cheering : there he stood, a broad-shouldered little man, with auburn hair and flowing whiskers framing a lined face which he himself has quite accurately described as stern, buttoned almost painfully into a tight-fitting grey frock coat, using very few gestures but pursuing the Grand Old Man through all the tortuosities of a long and complicated speech with the speed and accuracy of a bloodhound.

When, after 1895, Home Rule was buried for twenty years, Edward Clarke, though still the leader of the Bar and still a great parliamentary figure, became a little wayward, not to say independent in politics. He fought against his party

on the issues involved in the South African War
and resigned his seat at Plymouth. He fought
them again, four years later, on the question of
Tariff Reform, and resigned his seat as Member
for the City of London. But none of this made
any difference to the high regard in which he was
held by members of his own profession, by his
colleagues in Parliament, and by his multitude of
friends outside. He lived a long life in court and
senate, an example of courage, courtesy and untiring
industry to all who knew him ; and, although he
died many years after his public career was closed,
he has left behind him a delightful memory of a
Tory of the days of Mr. Disraeli.

OTHER FORE-MEN

(LIBERALS, ETC.)

SIR ROBERT REID*

1846–1923

To those of us who nursed the conceit that we
would soon know all the members of the House
of Commons by sight, the easier task was to
begin with the faces opposite to us rather than
with members of our own party. The Liberal
party had great men among them; of some of
them I have already written. Perhaps the most
popular of the others was ". Bob " Reid, who had
once kept wicket for Oxford University, had been
President of the M.C.C., and was now one of
the principal members of the team captained by
Sir William Harcourt against Lord Rosebery's
eleven. In private life the most charming and
affectionate of men, he was the " extremist " *par
excellence* when he spoke in the House of Commons.
Such was the depth of his party convictions that
every measure and every motive of his opponents
was, in his opinion, open to the gravest moral
censure. In vehemence of language, in fury of

* Created Earl Loreburn, 1911.

demeanour, neither William O'Brien nor Willie Redmond could rival him, and he scarcely ever spoke when he did not appear to be angry. It is not a little strange that â man, liable to such temperamental convulsions in the one House, should have made so equable a Lord Chancellor in the other; stranger still perhaps, that the furnace heat of his attacks never dissolved a particle of the friendships he had formed with those—and they were numberless on both sides of the House—who always called him " Bob."

MR. HALDANE*
1856–1928

HALDANE, a Rosebery-ite and a brother-Scot, was quite a different sort of Liberal—pale-faced, studious, rotund and quite imperturbable. Twenty years before people had begun to talk nonsense, at the beginning of the Great War, about his pro-German proclivities, George Curzon had nicknamed him " Schopenhauer "; and indeed, his whole appearance when he addressed the House of Commons— generally on some very abstruse legal or scientific subject—was that of a foreign philosopher lecturing his class at the University. He spoke generally without a note, in a high-pitched voice that never faltered; he paused neither for interruption nor applause; his only gestures were either a shrug

* Created Viscount Haldane, 1911.

VISCOUNT HALDANE

of his broad shoulders accompanied by a shake
of his head and a faintly deprecating smile, or
the outstretching of his hands with upturned
palms, as one who should say : " You see, it is
all as plain as a pikestaff." The truth is that
Haldane was far too clever for most of us ; but
the higher ranks of intelligence, like Arthur
Balfour and a few others, delighted in him. I
suppose that, in public life, he will be best remembered for his careful study of the German Army,
for his subsequent creation of an Expeditionary
Force in case of war and for his drastic reform of
the War Office. I never think of him as a great
party man, easily cajoled by Whips or colleagues,
or swayed by enthusiasm for any cause whatever.
All his conclusions had been arrived at and his
principles formed by dint of study in the cold
light of reason ; the human factor had very little,
if anything, to do with them. But in his private
capacity he was a changed man and very human
indeed ; with a passion for hard work and a corres-
ponding appetite for good company, plenty of
nourishment and large cigars. He gave one the
impression of never having known a day's illness
or a day's worry in his life, of complete content-
ment and perfect self-confidence. These are good
qualities in a friend and in a career. Haldane
had a host of friends, men and women ; and
at least three careers : philosopher, lawyer and

statesman. He had, I suppose, gained the highest prizes attainable in all of them when he died.

MR. BRYCE*

1838–1922

JAMES BRYCE, yet another Scotsman, was a veteran Liberal who served his party with great distinction, but whose influence in the House of Commons was not as great as it was in the wider world outside. For Bryce was not, I think, a politician by nature or by preference; but he had a generous and sentimental nature that urged him into battle against the " Bulgarian atrocities " in the closing days of Mr. Disraeli, and in favour of Irish Home Rule which kept him very near to Mr. Gladstone's side. If a man is really necessary in British politics, it is much easier for him to get into the House of Commons than to get out of it; and Bryce, with his enthusiasms and encyclopaedic knowledge, was of great and constant assistance to his party. But though his head was for forty years at the disposal of his colleagues, his heart must often have strayed far away from the green benches upon which he was compelled to sit. He was a very many-sided man who, in his day, had travelled extensively, read omnivorously and knew everyone of any intellectual importance or high

* Created Viscount Bryce, 1914.

attainment during the latter half of his life. He was also an author of international fame which may be said to have begun at Oxford with his Arnold Essay on " The Holy Roman Empire," and to have culminated, long years afterwards, with his justly celebrated " History of the American Commonwealth." One can imagine that it was an immense deprivation to him to give up his life of physical activity (for, *inter alia*, he was a noted Alpine-climber) and of mental enjoyment in order to look after the affairs of one or other of the Departments of State in surroundings where he did not really shine. Perhaps he was a little too didactic, too abstract, too omniscient, for the House of Commons ; perhaps his habit of pointing and wagging his beard* (as Haldane used to point and wag his finger) at the Opposition got on the nerves of some people, and the mechanical raising and lowering of his rugged bushy eyebrows whilst speaking worried others. Nor was he very easy to listen to, especially for long—brevity was not his strongest suit—but his speeches were always full of information as became a Regius Professor of Civil Law and of Jurisprudence. At dinner, or in walking home from the House, his conversation was indescribably varied. General knowledge was his province, but detailed information on out

---

* Mr. Gladstone used to say chaffingly : " As for Bryce, his beard is an insult."

N

of-the-way subjects was his speciality. Nothing
came amiss to him; and his prodigious memory
retained it all, from the cut of Alcibiades' hair
to the measurements of Napoleon's bedstead.
Alfred Lyttelton once observed that Arthur Balfour's
talk was the butter of conversation, but that John
Morley's was the bread. I agree, and feel inclined
to add that Bryce's was the crust; crisp, and
concealing no end of nourishment.

The appointment of Bryce to be our Ambassador
at Washington was a feather in Campbell-Bannerman's cap. It released him from Ireland, where
we may think what we like of his administration,
and promoted him to a sphere where his name was
already a household word and where he was
entirely in his element. He was hospitable, accessible, omniscient, and he adored talking. All of
these qualities combined in the representative of
a friendly Power made Mr. Bryce *persona gratissima*
to the American people. He travelled widely
throughout the country and made himself familiar
with its new conditions; I know not how many
Universities he visited nor upon how many subjects
he delivered addresses. But I do know that we
have to thank him, perhaps most of all, for bringing
the United States and Canada into those closer
and more intimate relations which now exist
between them, and which redound to the advantage
of both countries. On his return from the States

in 1918 he was made a Peer and, although always an Elder Statesman in the councils of his party, he took a less prominent place in the political life of England.   It is generally believed, I know not with how much truth, that he was the counsellor and at the right hand of those whose privilege it is to advise His Majesty with regard to his public pronouncements, and these utterances were of supreme value and importance during the critical days of War.   If he was that counsellor, or even part-author of those inspiring calls to duty, let us commend him very highly for his share in them.   They teach us how a man, released from party controversy and retired from the responsible duty of representing his country abroad, may forget his prejudices, ripen his opinions, widen his outlook and use his experience, knowledge and scholarship for the service of the Common-wealth.

MR. LEWIS HARCOURT*

1863–1922

IN an earlier chapter of this book I have given my impressions of Sir William Harcourt; but so far nothing has been said of his son, " Loulou," his right hand man during the last thirty years of his life, and the champion strategist and tac-tician of the Liberal party from 1890 to 1906 whilst

* Created Viscount Harcourt, 1917.

they were wandering in the wilderness. Far
transcending his political ambitions, his love of
luxury and his pleasure in sport and society, was
Lewis Harcourt's absorbing devotion to his father ;
the offer of a lucrative office under Government
or of a seat in the House of Commons could not
tempt him to abandon the post of private secretary
to Sir William, nor the power that he wielded behind
his official leader's throne. But, when his father
decided in 1902 to stand no more for Parliament,
and Loulou knew that he was passionately anxious
for his son to carry on his name there, then filial
piety compelled him to fight a by-election and
he was returned as Liberal member for Rossendale
in 1904. I well remember the day when he was
introduced to the House, by the Liberal Whip
on one side of him and the commanding figure
of his fine old father on the other. The ranks
of Tuscany cheered indiscriminately with their
opponents, and Sir William wrote : " the dearest
hope of my life was fulfilled. The House was
crowded on both sides, and both equally cheered
the rising and the setting sun."

Thus heartened, the " Eminence Grise " of the
Liberals stepped confidently out of the shadow
into the limelight of the political stage, with whose
coulisses he was as familiar as with the corridors
in his own house.

Loulou was one of the Dandies of his time ;

VISCOUNT HARCOURT
with his daughters

very tall, hatchet-faced, roman-nosed and most carefully dressed. I had known him from my Eton days when he belonged to a small coterie of *virtuosi*, of whom the late Lord Esher was the chief, who made it their principal pleasure to keep young by associating themselves closely with the masters and boys of their old school and talking to us of the beauties and the duties of the greater world outside in which we were soon to join them. They posed as gentlemen of leisure, half cynics and half aesthetes, who had nothing particular to do in life; we little knew how hard most of them worked under the disguise of *dilettanti*. But those who were better acquainted with him realised what a tremendous appetite for work, what inflexible will-power, was hidden beneath the brim of Loulou's immaculate tall hat. He had the politics of a Danton, the manner of Count D'Orsay, and the artistic flair of a Duveen : a strange mixture of qualities to bring into the rather sombre *galère* of Campbell-Bannerman's Cabinet. But his silken address and his golden gift of silence were of great advantage to his party, which was only looking for the earliest opportunity of making full use of them. A year passed, and he was honoured by a high post in C.-B.'s administration as First Commissioner of Works, and by a Privy Councillorship to boot. In that capacity he made his maiden speech in the House of Commons, and he

made his mark as well. His voice was gentle,
his enunciation careful and his manner of delivery
was persuasive and distinguished. In the smoking-
room he was an admirable "mixer," with a genius
for making friends; and in his Department his
artistic knowledge and conservative instincts (not
politics) were of high value to the country in general
and to London in particular. So that nobody
was surprised when, in 1910, he was promoted
to the Colonial Office: a position which he occupied
as Secretary of State for five years, during which
time his long and exhaustive annual summaries
of progress in our Dominions and Crown Colonies
(on the occasion of presenting Colonial Office
estimates) provide a series of the best speeches
that I heard in the House of Commons.

With the War his active political life ended—
far too soon—and he was not included in Mr.
Asquith's first Coalition Cabinet. Soon afterwards
he was translated to the House of Lords; but most
of his time was devoted to Nuneham, which he
had inherited from his father, and to duties connected with the British Museum, the National
Portrait Gallery and the Wallace Collection, of
all of which he was a Trustee. It was a sheer joy
to stay with him at Nuneham, where both house
and garden became more comfortable and more
beautiful during every year of his occupancy,

thanks to the combined taste and knowledge of himself and of his accomplished and charming wife. At last he had time to indulge in his hobby of horticulture in the spring and summer, and to entertain delightful parties during the shooting season. He was a first-rate shot, and managed his partridge-driving with rare skill. Two things he especially required of his keepers, quiet and speed : so everything ran like clockwork, including the teams of black cocker spaniels which were stationed behind each gun. If he had lived, I am sure that he would have been a distinguished writer on art and political subjects, for he was an assiduous student and amassed new knowledge every day in his fine library at Nuneham. But I am not so certain that he would have remained a Radical.

MR. JOHN REDMOND

1851–1918

MEN might come and men might go ; Governments might become the Opposition and these, in their turn, might fill the seats of the mighty ; but John Redmond always occupied the corner seat on the top bench below the gangway on the Opposition side of the House during the generation that I sat in it. He looked exactly what he was : a descendant of an old Irish family with considerable property ; a man trained in the law and later as a

Clerk in the House of Commons, who had learned all its rules and had designedly broken some of them; but who conducted himself, even in his misconduct, with unvarying decorum, and frowned with unconcealed disgust when the more uproarious of his followers created an unparliamentary " divarshun." When it was the fashion to wear frockcoats in the House, as it was thirty years ago, Redmond wore one too; when some unknown *arbiter elegantiarum* relaxed that rule, Redmond bowed to it and appeared in " tails " or in a morning jacket, but always wearing a bunch of violets. There he sat, his hands folded across his waistcoat, always alert—now listening to the speaker (if he thought it worth while), now keeping a watchful eye upon his fiery team which was generally docile enough in the division lobbies, though they were seldom all contented at the same time with their leader. Few men would have endured the caprices of his followers for so long as John Redmond did; there was no bed of roses for an Irish leader after the deposition of Mr. Parnell. But through good and evil report, with a few short intervals, he was the acknowledged chief of the Irish party and became, between 1910 and 1912, something like the dictator of the House of Commons; for, by the votes that he could command, the Liberal party was condemned to stand or fall as he required.

There is no doubt but that he was a great speaker, one of the best in the House ; but he was not an Irish orator. He could not rid himself of a steady Whig character, which shunned the exhibition of emotion and of unrestrained speech. Parnell had been an iceberg, alike to friend and foe, with considerable success. Redmond copied him and, time and again, his measured and dignified, almost abstract, contributions to an Irish debate at a critical moment cooled the atmosphere and averted one of those collisions with the Chair or with the Government which he loathed. This gift of reducing fever heat in an assembly such as the House of Commons is a rare one ; Lord Hartington and Arthur Balfour had it; so had Sir Edward Grey, and they displayed it in different ways : Lord Hartington, by adopting a weary reflective tone of voice which had a calming and soporific tendency ; Arthur Balfour, by referring rather casually to the bone of contention and then proceeding to talk quite naturally and charmingly about something else ; Sir Edward's method was the application of the ice-pack of close reasoning and impartial analysis. I wonder whether the House of Commons has ever consciously realised what it owes to such men and to their psychological intuitions which preserve it from scenes, the frequent repetition of which must inevitably damage the prestige and reputation of our

Parliament in the eyes of England and of the world.
I never heard John Redmond throw fuel on the
flames of debate. He belonged more to the school
of parliamentary orators of the line of Burke. He
might have been goaded by the jeers of William
O'Brien or by the sub-acid jibes of Tim Healy;
he might have been roused by the inadequacy of
the Home Rule proposals of the Liberals or enraged
by the adamant idolatry of the Union by the
Conservatives : his method was always the same.
He never replied on the spur of the moment. His
practice was to retire to his private room whilst
the debate proceeded, and then to return armed
with a sheaf of notes from which he proceeded
to declaim, in a resonant voice and in classical
English, his answer to the arguments of his opponents and to reiterate the points of his own policy.
Whilst listening to him, and I heard most of his
great speeches after 1895, he always impressed me ;
but I do not think that, even if I had been an anti-
Parnellite or a wavering Unionist, he could ever
have convinced or converted me. What were
his limitations ? Well ; that apparent lack of
spontaneity which comes from adhering closely
to written notes was one ; his real or assumed
lack of enthusiasm was another ; his surprising
lack of humour was a third—all of these so foreign
to the peculiar gifts of his fellow-countrymen,
whether they were exhibited by Colonel Saunderson,

Mr. W. Redmond

[Sport and General

the leader of the Ulster Unionists, or by his brother Willie Redmond—the drollest, most obstreperous and kindliest of Nationalists—for whom I had great affection. He was killed in 1917, fighting with the Irish Division in the Great War.

John Redmond died the year afterwards in 1918. He had put his hand to the Home Rule plough in 1880 and he lived to see its work accomplished, after nearly two generations, in 1914. When War broke out we knew another Redmond. His claim for Ireland satisfied, he was genuinely whole-hearted in the defence of the Empire. He threw the mass of his great influence in Ireland into recruiting, and denounced as " pro-Germans and shirkers " those who did not flock to the colours. A great believer in voluntary effort inspired by National feeling, he tried hard to have an Irish Division in the British Army. I happened to meet him one day in the War Office, after we had had separate talks with Lord Kitchener, and I shall always remember his dejection of spirit as he told me that his proposal had been turned down. He was a very single-hearted man. He declined to take Cabinet office from Mr. Asquith in his first Coalition Government for reasons which I appreciate without fully understanding them. He condemned that insensate revolution in Dublin in Easter Week, 1916, and never forgave himself for not having known of it, and, if possible, prevented it.

I do not honestly think that whilst I was in Parliament I could have written, as I now do, so impartially of John Redmond, who found it difficult to make friends with any of us on this side of St. George's Channel. His brother Willie was different; we became great personal allies, and often exchanged live grouse to try to bring new blood into Ireland and Scotland. But, after all, John Redmond was a great parliamentarian, a fine character, and made history for his native land. He it was who got for Irish Nationalism what it said it wanted; let us hope that the Irish Free State will never forget him.

MR. T. M. HEALY

1855–1931

THE task of writing these recollections of statesmen and politicians who have passed away but who, in their time, were my chiefs or fellow-members or friends is a task that is tinged with sadness. I had thought it was concluded and, indeed, this book had already been submitted to my publisher when the melancholy news reached me that " Tim Healy " —as he was known the wide world over—had died. Incomplete as this volume admittedly is, it would have been even more seriously lacking if I had not included in it this sketch of a friend of mine whose life was lived far more in the storm than in the sunshine; a lone, lurid yet lovable figure in the House of Commons between the years 1880 and 1918; a man who passed from being known as "the street arab of Parliament" to the honourable dignity of Governor-General of the Irish Free State.

The biographer who writes Tim Healy's life will have to describe the career of a patriotic unparliamentary firework. He could dazzle with his wit, amaze with the beauty of his eloquence, scorch with the sparks of his burning irony, splutter and hiss in paroxysms of savage indignation and invective, rise suddenly to great heights of knowledge or descend, with equal rapidity, to depths of personal abuse. Very few men in my time, who were not leading occupants of the front benches in Parliament, could be relied upon to "fill the House" when they rose to speak. Sir Edward Clarke was one, Hugh Cecil was another, and "Tim" was, perhaps, the greatest draw of all. The uncertainty of him was his charm; you never knew in what mood you would find him, for he would curse or coo just as the spirit moved him. In my early parliamentary years the bitterest of his battles inside the ranks of the Irish party were more or less over, though he had not forgotten his role of *Athanasius contra mundum*.

as when he described the Nationalist section in
Parliament as " two united Irish parties in the
House, and *I'm one of them*." He had served
Parnell first as private secretary, then as a brilliant
supporter; finally he had the largest share in
driving his erstwhile chief out of public life when
the Divorce Court had decided against him. " We
shall soon see who is to be the master in Ireland,"
said Parnell arrogantly during one of the turbulent
debates in Committee Room 15 ; and Tim hissed
at him, " The question is, who is to be the mistress " ;
a *double entendre* whose wit was extinguished by
its inextricable venom. That was one aspect of
the sombre man with the ardent rebel heart of
a patriotic Nationalist who, nevertheless, had
decided sympathies for the British monarchy and
the British Parliament, so long as they kept their
hands off Ireland. We shall not easily forget his
defence of our reigning Sovereign against the
slanders uttered by some of his more violent fellow-
countrymen : " There is one thing to be said about
this ' foreign king,' and that is that he is a gentleman and we know his pedigree. I wish we knew
as much about those who talk of his interference
in Irish affairs." And, for all his snapping and
sniping, he really liked being in Parliament and
thoroughly enjoyed speaking there. " To me, it
is as amusing as going to a music-hall," he said
to me once, when he had made a particularly success-

ful and witty speech. He had an appearance and a manner in addressing the House which were all his own : that rather saturnine visage, as of a bearded crow with spectacles which shielded a pair of piercing eyes, and a mouth that twisted into strange shapes when he was angry ; that baggy morning coat whose large side pockets bulged with parliamentary papers ; those short bow-legs. To protect his eyes he usually wore a silk hat, and this he would reverently remove and place upon the seat beside him when he got up to speak. Then, plunging his hands deep into his trouser-pockets and, as somebody once said, gnashing his teeth at the Mace, he would begin in a voice that could scarcely be heard until he warmed to his subject. One remembers so many of the good things that he said : once he enquired innocently, having received an answer as to the number of horses and mules transported from England for the South African War—" And how many *asses* ? " On another occasion he interrupted a rather tedious speech on some Franchise Bill, when the late Sir George Bartley informed the House that he represented a very dense constit-uency: "A clear case of natural selection," ejacu-lated Tim. And he was the same in the Four Courts, brilliant and unexpected. I forget the nature of the case which that stony-hearted advocate James Campbell, K.C. (later Lord Glenavy, who

died but a few days before him) was arguing with
so much emotion that the tears streamed down his
face : " The greatest miracle since Moses struck
the rock " observed Healy to the jury when he
came to reply. But the speech which I shall
always remember as one of the most eloquent to
which I ever listened was delivered by him in
defence of denominational schools during the
passage of Mr. Balfour's Education Bill. With
all his " corrosive humour and diabolical irony,"
Tim was a deeply religious man, who was stirred
to the depths of his being by the speeches of those
who argued against State support of religious
education in our schools. I am glad that *The
Times*, in its obituary notice of him, has revived
the memory of one part of this beautiful piece
of true oratory : he quivered as he delivered it
in a tense voice : we were thrilled as we listened :

" I would rather have my children learn to
say " Our Father " than learn the use of the
globes. I would rather that they understood their
religion in the provision for the eternity which
is to come than that they should become rich
and prosperous, and educated in the things
of this world. I give very little for your
education. I cannot spell myself. I cannot
parse an English sentence. I cannot do the rule
of three. I am supposed to know a little law,

but I think that is a mistake. But if there is one thing which I and mine have got a grip of, it is the belief in the Infinite Christ to come ; the conviction that our children, whatever be their distresses, whatever be their misfortunes, whatever be their poverty in this world, if they have listened to the teaching of the Church, will reap a rich reward in putting into practice the lessons of Christianity which they receive in the Catholic school."

There, in that speech, was all the same courage of conviction that led him so often to extremes of violence of language against policies and old friends, all the simplicity and candour for which he might be loved or hated, all the fervour and eloquence which caused him to be feared, envied and admired.

It was no ordinary man who could turn, as though in a night, from being the old weather-beaten stormy petrel of Parliament in general and of Nationalist Ireland in particular, to becoming the acclaimed representative of His Majesty as the first Governor-General of the Irish Free State, a post which he occupied with dignity and con-spicuous success during five eventful and experi-mental years. Old friends from this country who stayed with him at Viceregal Lodge were full of

o

praise of the dignified simplicity, the courtesy and
charm of his hospitality towards all of his guests.
In truth, they could have asked for no better company
than their host, whose anecdotes, inimitably told
with the dry fragrance of an old vintage, ranged
from the days " when I was in gaol " to scenes
in the House of Commons and the vicissitudes
which led him to the throne of honour in Dublin
Castle. " What a change," said a quondam
member of an ex-Viceroy's staff, surveying the
Governor's modest establishment with a critical but
very friendly eye : " in my time Viceregal Lodge
was staffed with Colonels and Captains and other
military swells." Tim Healy smiled—the female
servants had left the room—and replied, " But
my staff is much more elegant ; they are all hereditary
' generals '."

Of Tim in private life others will speak with
far more intimate knowledge than can I. Yet
I want to record his unvarying kindness to me,
which lasted through years of bitter political
strife down to a few years ago when I begged
him to get some autographs for me. " Here they
are," he wrote ; " I have had some of them translated, for they are written in Erse which you don't
understand ; no more do I." If we were discussing
books or Church schools or purely constitutional
questions, he shed his politics like a garment
and at once became the friendliest, most genial,

[Sport and General

MR. T. M. HEALY

on an Irish race-course

most helpful and informative of colleagues. I
agree with all those who have declared that to
dine alone with Tim Healy was a feast to remember
as a great occasion. Men like James Campbell,
to whom I have already referred, and Edward
Carson, with whom he fought many a bitter
campaign at Westminster and before juries, said
the same thing. Carson once told me that, after
some big fight on the Northern Circuit in Ireland,
he and Tim sat next one another at dinner and
split a bottle of old Burgundy. They had a great
evening together, and at last Carson said "Why
is it, Tim, do you suppose, that in spite of all
our quarrels we are always such good friends?"
Healy's melancholy answer surprised him: "Can
it be because we are both such thundering black-
guards?" A rhetorical figure of cynical speech;
but, wherever the truth may lie, this will be found
embedded in it: that although Tim Healy had
a genius for making enemies he had an astonishing
gift for making friends in the most unexpected
quarters. I saw enough of him to understand
that he must have been almost an impossible man
to work with in a political party; vain, prejudiced,
ambitious and quick-tempered. That was whilst
his lone hand was fighting for the lead. But when
he "arrived" in 1922 and became Governor of
the Free State, the uncrowned "Monarch of all
he surveyed," all those unattractive defects dis-

appeared and he worked like a slave for the success
of the new adventure. What he achieved was
generously acknowledged by President Cosgrave
who declared, at the end of Healy's Governorship,
that out of welter and strife had come security
and peace, and that the Governor-General had
sustained his position with high dignity and
exalted courage.

THE HOUSE OF COMMONS
1895–1905

No young man of my time whose ambition and talents pointed to a Parliamentary career could have developed them in a nicer House of Commons than that which assembled after the General Election of 1895.

The novice comes reverently and thankfully to the knee of the Mother of Parliaments with the feelings of a new boy about to enter a famous public school, mixed with those of a seafarer who has come safely into port at last. He is anxious to get his bearings and to learn the language and the laws of this new country in which he hopes to live and make his name; he is diffidently curious to see its rulers and to mark the behaviour of its inhabitants of whom he has read and heard so much.

The '95 Parliament, so it seemed to us, teemed with celebrities who were giants in their day: there were those who, like Harcourt and Morley, had stood and fought by Gladstone's side in the battle for Home Rule; there were the doughty champions of the Union—Salisbury, Goschen and

Devonshire, Balfour, Chamberlain and Hicks-Beach,
who had defied the Grand Old Man and won.
It was something of a minor disappointment to
us that we had just missed the honour of belonging
to the same House of Commons as Mr. Gladstone
and Lord Randolph Churchill, and that we could
not claim to have sat under the august presidency
of Mr. Speaker Peel, whose eagle eye and nicely
calculated stammer were the terror of the evil-
doer. But there were compensations, rich compensations, in the residuum that was left; we
could claim that we sat in Parliament with Mr.
Villiers, who was an M.P. when Queen Victoria
was crowned; we were interested spectators in
the open competition between John Redmond and
Tim Healy for the leadership of the Irish party,
which had not been decided by the vitriolic debates
in Committee Room 15; we witnessed the rise
and fall of the Harcourt republic, a struggle between
the old Gladstonians and the followers of Lord
Rosebery for the hegemony of the Liberal party
which ended in an indeterminate victory for Sir
Henry Campbell-Bannerman: we noted the pugna-
cious and unfaltering ascent of Lloyd George up
the ladder of parliamentary fame, and we applauded
with increasing enthusiasm the mastery and charm
which distinguished Arthur Balfour as Leader of
the House. All of these things made history,
although we did not know it at the time. And

then we sat at the feet of the "busy B's," Sir Frederick Banbury, Sir George Trout Barclay, and "Tommy" Bowles, to learn the twin sciences of parliamentary procedure and orderly obstruction of business which this trio had developed into a fine Art. No others could hold a candle to them on this stage, the only stage upon which Government Whips allowed their followers to strut. These very capable men had, in their turn, learned the tricks of this trade from the Irish benches, but had greatly improved upon those earlier and cruder methods ; so that, by comparison, it was almost painful to watch the old-fashioned antics of Swift McNeill and William O'Brien, or the inartistic and amateur attempts of Jimmy Caldwell and Mr. Weir—two very dour Scotsmen—to throw their spoonfuls of sand into the parliamentary clockwork. We had some good light comedians, too, with "Labby" and Sir Wilfrid Lawson, Frank Lockwood and Colonel Saunderson (both of them first-rate caricaturists) at the head of that list, an admirable counterfoil to the encyclo-paedic profundities of James Bryce and of Sir Charles Dilke with his infant school of doctrinaire Radicals. We heard W. H. Lecky make his maiden speech, towering from a back bench high above his fellows, and speaking most perfect English in a rapid, rueful falsetto, wringing his hands and genuflecting to the Chair as if in abject apology

for daring to address that earthly throne of grace ;
he and Augustine Birrell (who once told me that
he seldom read a book in the House of Commons
and never understood one) showed us by their
speeches how to appreciate literature in language,
and to value at their proper worth the polished
contributions of Professors Butcher and Jebb in
the succeeding Parliament. It is difficult, thirty-
five years afterwards, to remember the names of
all the curious characters who abounded in that
House of Commons ; there was William Johnson
of Ballykilbeg, with the appearance and asceticism
of an Orange minor prophet, who protested against
the Popish practice of adjourning the House on
Ascension Day ; there was a heavy, soft-spoken
London solicitor called Sydney Gedge, who used
to pound down daily to Westminster from Mitcham
on a tricycle ; a popular fox-hunting squire from
Warwickshire, named Muntz, who once electrified
the House by entering it in a pink dress-coat after
a hunt dinner ; Sir Benjamin Stone too, always
kodak in hand, whose expert work in photography
has provided many albums of rare parliamentary
pictures for the House of Commons ; Charlie
Beresford, the popular representative of the Navy,
whose breeziness was a joy for ever ; " Jim "
Lowther, the bed-rock and last fortress of Tory
Protection and the Corn Laws, with his trusty
lieutenants, Harry Chaplin (also an eminent patron

of the Turf) and Sir Howard Vincent, whose vocal " asides " were more penetrating than most people's loudest efforts in the open air. Nor must I forget a kindly and patriotic old Irishman, J. F. X. O'Brien, whom we viewed with great interest as the last British subject who had been sentenced to be " hanged, drawn and quartered "—a penalty which Hugh Cecil and I once designed for Keir Hardie, but the law was " agin " us !; Michael Davitt, the Fenian, with a long prison record behind him, but in private life " the mildest mannered man who ever scuttled a ship " ; and Doctor Tanner (also from Ireland) whose sobriety was not his strongest point, but many of whose intemperate and unparliamentary ejaculations were extremely witty. One of them I always remember as a gem : he was being taken to task in the Lobby for his indecorous behaviour by Ashmead Bartlett, a genial swashbuckler on the Conservative side ; and he made reply : " Ah, Ashmead ; ah, Bartlett ! I shall be sober to-morrow, but you will still be a——fool ! " Yes ; it was a delightful House in which to start one's parliamentary life ; all its members were kind and considerate to us new-comers on whichever side of the House we sat ; the fires of Home Rule, which had kindled a free fight in Parliament only two years before, had almost died out, and no new question had arisen to embitter discussion ; once more we were a happy

family at Westminster, at least until the opening
of the Boer War when the flames of party conflict
once more leaped up and gave us a taste of what
our predecessors had known *sub consule Gladstone.*
The unity of the Conservative party was hardly
affected by the war; but the Liberals developed
the already existing fissure; and C.B. with Harcourt
and Morley and their followers turned angry
backs upon Grey, Asquith, Haldane, and the rest
of the " Lib-Imps " with Lord Rosebery at their
head. The new Election in 1900, at the height of
the war-fever, returned a House that was " out
for blood " in one direction or another. For no
sooner was peace declared with the Boers in 1902
than Tariff Reform broke out, shattered the unity
of the Unionist party and, ultimately, drove its
scattered companies into the wilderness for nearly
twenty years. It was undoubtedly a more interesting
Parliament than its predecessor: it was the last
Parliament of Queen Victoria's reign and the
first of King Edward VII; it recorded the resignation of Lord Salisbury as Prime Minister and the
end of our foreign policy of splendid isolation,
which made way for alliances with France, Japan,
and, subsequently, with Russia; it saw the passage
of Mr. Balfour's Education Bill and of George
Wyndham's great Land Purchase Act for Ireland;
and, as I have said, it offered in its declining years
the melancholy spectacle of the utter disintegration

of the Cabinet that had brought these historic things to pass. Its personnel was not so very different to that of the last Parliament: Hugh Cecil, incomparably the cleverest of the young men elected in '95 (if we except Alfred Lyttelton —a much older man—who was destined for a short but stormy career as Colonial Secretary from 1903 to 1905), was already in the first flight cf parliamentary orators; Harry Percy, who would have become Duke of Northumberland if he had lived, was appointed Under-Secretary for India in Mr. Balfour's first Administration—a " stipendiary echo ", as he was chaffingly described at a mock trial to decide whether he was a fit and proper person to remain in our small independent Order of Hughligans. He was a great loss to the party and to the country, and his death was sincerely mourned on both sides of the House of Commons. Among the new members we welcomed Winston Churchill, fresh from his adventures in the Boer War, which he had been describing daily and nightly to trans-Atlantic audiences; for three brief years he elected to sit beside us on the Tory benches, but Tariff Reform drove him with others across the floor of the House into the arms of the Radicals, with whom he stayed until, having reached the age of discretion, he escaped from them and returned to the faith of his father. Bonar Law, about whom I have written at length elsewhere

in this book, came almost unnoticed as a recruit
to this Parliament, and Harry Cust, the popular,
good-looking and brilliant editor of the *Pall Mall
Gazette*, was another promising addition to our
party, though the promise was never quite fulfilled.
This leads me to note that in the 1900 Parliament
the Press was very fully represented in the House
of Commons. Besides Cust and Churchill (the
latter an intrepid war correspondent in several
campaigns, despite his youth) we had Leonard
Courtney, a portentously solemn old gentleman
who had been a leader-writer on *The Times* in
his early days ; Sir Edward Clarke who passed in
due course from the Press Gallery to the post of
Solicitor-General under Lord Salisbury, and T. P.
O'Connor, the brilliant Irish orator, who must
have owned and contributed more words to more
newspapers than any other man living during his
time. Besides these we had Labouchere, proprietor
and editor of *Truth*, Tommy Bowles the owner
of *Vanity Fair*, one Horner of the *Whitehall Review*,
and Arthur Eliot, who for a short time edited
the *Edinburgh Review*. In all there were over thirty
journalists returned to the House, which included
among its members Harry Lawson, of the *Daily
Telegraph*, C. P. Scott (*Manchester Guardian*), Wilcox
of the *Liverpool Courier*, Sir John Lang (*Dundee
Advertiser*) Sir George Newnes (*Westminster Gazette*),
and at least one Harmsworth. It may be for this

reason that the proceedings of Parliament were so fully reported in those days, when far more space was devoted not only to important speeches at Westminster and in the country but also to Lobby gossip, often quite interesting in character. On the other hand, it may be that public taste has changed and that, in the rush and hurry of life nowadays, nobody has time or inclination to read more than is absolutely necessary about politics, although everybody, male and female, is anxious to have a vote—and nearly everybody has got one. One hesitates to suggest that, in the first Parliament of this century, politics were more interesting (at least from a spectacular point of view) and the characteristics of our leading politicians more arresting than they are to-day ; for one is always prone to believe that events in which one took part oneself, and colleagues with whom one worked, were of infinitely greater importance than subsequent events and politicians with whose development one is less intimately concerned. Be all this as it may, I for one—who happen nowadays to be among those who spend much time out of England and seldom go to the House of Commons —miss the parliamentary sketches, from pens like those of " Toby M.P." and of T. P. O'Connor, which illustrated with good-natured satire and deep parliamentary knowledge the strength and the weaknesses of the men who played the principal and minor parts in the comedies staged week by week at Westminster. For I have no hesitation in saying, after over twenty years' experience of that particular play-house, that there is no theatre comparable with the House of Commons, nor are there any comedies more instinct with human interest than those performed within its walls. There you are provided, as in some Pirandello plays, with actors and audience upon the same stage, with plots that develop before your eyes, sometimes into tragedy and sometimes into farce : only the scenario is sketched out beforehand ; no libretto exists, for the text depends upon the impromptu skill of the actors on the stage at the moment. A full-dress debate in Parliament is the finest human comedy that I want to see, where the principal characters can by their words change and sway the fate of millions, and where the audience is the most expert and the fairest in the world.